Hong Kong English

May Wong

Hong Kong English

Exploring Lexicogrammar and Discourse
from a Corpus-Linguistic Perspective

May Wong
School of English
University of Hong Kong
Pok Fu Lam, Hong Kong

ISBN 978-1-137-51963-4   ISBN 978-1-137-51964-1   (eBook)
DOI 10.1057/978-1-137-51964-1

Library of Congress Control Number: 2017930569

This Palgrave Pivot imprint is published by Springer Nature
The registered company is Macmillan Publishers Ltd.
The registered company address is: The Campus, 4 Crinan Street, London, N1 9XW, United Kingdom

For Arthur

Acknowledgements

This book owes a great deal to a great many people. It is not possible to name everyone who has made a contribution to it in some way or another but I hope, at least, you will know my thanks.

This book was begun while working at the Department of Linguistics and completed while working at the School of English, both in the University of Hong Kong. I am exceedingly grateful to both units for the time and space afforded to me that has enabled this project to be pursued to fruition.

The intellectual space at the intersection between Corpus Linguistics and World Englishes has only relatively recently been opened. I am grateful to all those researchers who have had a hand in creating his highly productive space and whose work is reflected in this book. I am especially grateful to those people working in this area with whom I have been able to exchange ideas by distance or at international conferences, meetings and symposia. Particular thanks are due to Dr Vincent Ooi.

At the University of Hong Kong, I have always found an environment that is extremely warm and supportive, both personally and professionally. I am grateful to colleagues there for making me feel so at home. This book has benefitted enormously from the many stimulating conversations I have had with my colleagues, especially Dr Janny Leung and Dr Dirk Noël, at the School of English. While at the Department of Linguistics I enjoyed numerous discussions on matters of linguistics in general and Cantonese linguistics in particular with both my colleagues and postgraduate students. Special thanks go to Professor Kang-Kwong Luke and Dr Richard Xiao who have helped me in various capacities over the years with this work. I am also grateful to two anonymous reviewers for reading draft chapters and offering useful suggestions for improvement. All remaining oversights are, of course, my own responsibility.

I owe a great deal of gratitude to Professor Tony McEnery who introduces me to the vast and exciting field of corpus linguistics by being my PhD supervisor at Lancaster University. I am very grateful to Dr Paul Rayson for offering me a free account to access the online corpus analysis interface Wmatrix. I would like to thank Professor Gerald Nelson for kindly granting me a licence to use the Hong Kong component of the International Corpus of English in my research. I would also like to thank the following for permission to reuse previously published material in my book:

- De Gruyter Mouton, for 'Hong Kong English' in Bernd Kortmann and Kerstin Lunkenheimer (eds.) *The Mouton World Atlas of Variation in English*, Berlin and New York, Mouton de Gruyter, pp. 548–561, 2012 (Chap. 1).
- Elsevier, for 'Expressions of gratitude by Hong Kong speakers of English: Research from the International Corpus of English in Hong Kong (ICE-HK)' in *Journal of Pragmatics* 42 (5): 1243–1257, 2010 (Chap. 4).

Earlier versions of Chaps. 2 and 3 were previously published by Taylor & Francis as 'Tag questions in Hong Kong English: A corpus-based study' in *Asian Englishes* 10 (1): 44–61, 2007 (Chap. 2), and '*Committee, staff, council*, etc.: A corpus analysis of collective nouns in Hong Kong English' in *Asian Englishes* 12 (1): 4–19, 2009 (Chap. 3).

At the publishers, I would like to thank all those involved for commissioning the work and for so efficiently handling the production process.

Always last but never least, I would like to thank Arthur, my shining light, for the love and support that he has shown me over the years and for his patience during the final stages of preparing the manuscript for this book. I hope somehow I will be able to repay him.

Contents

List of Figures

List of Tables

1

Hong Kong English: An Overview

Abstract Wong offers a much-need summary of the sociocultural background of Hong Kong English (HKE) and the profile of its structural features. Focussing on lexicogrammar, the chapter also draws attention to features relating to pronouns and nouns, tense and redundant grammatical elements and uses a typological perspective to facilitate a better understanding of substrate influence from Cantonese. As well as looking at the ways in which HKE has emerged, Wong explores the methodological implications of corpus linguistics in World-Englishes research. 'The profile of structural features in Hong Kong English' concludes with a brief overview of detailed case studies of different aspects of this variety of English undertaken in the subsequent chapters of the book *Hong Kong English: Exploring Lexicogrammar and Discourse from a Corpus-Linguistic Perspective*.

Keywords Socio-cultural background of Hong Kong English • Corpus linguistics • ICE-HK • Structural features • Typological profile • Substrate influence

1.1   Introduction

Situated on China's south coast and being a former British colony, Hong Kong is renowned for its 'East meets West' tradition in which English and Cantonese are the two main languages of the city. This language situation has created the conditions for Hong Kong English (HKE) to become a newly emerging, nativised variety of English. As Joseph remarks, HKE is 'well along the path of emergence' (2004, p. 139) and growing recognition 'will be a future development' (2004, p. 149). In fact, the status of the variety has been hotly disputed over the years. Some twenty years ago Luke and Richards (1982, p. 55) denied the existence of a distinct 'Hong Kong English' variety in favour of clearly exonormatively oriented 'English in Hong Kong'. This attitude has been widely supported by teachers and linguists alike in the 1990s (Li 1999, p. 95; Tsui and Bunton 2000; Pang 2003). However, the role and status of the English language in Hong Kong is now being revalued and redefined after a seminal work edited by Bolton (2002) was published on the subject. As Bolton (2003, p. 50) suggests, the label 'Hongkong English' first appeared in an article of the South China Morning Post—a local English newspaper—published in 1987, highlighting the fact that the variety is an 'incipient patois' and it 'cannot avoid absorbing the characteristics of the vernacular, especially one as vibrant as Cantonese [i.e. the native language of Hong Kong people]'.

While English is acquired through formal classroom instruction as a second/foreign language (i.e. an L2 variety type in this questionnaire), as Gisborne (2009, p. 150) rightly points out, 'it is not fair to state that HKE is a simple L2 variety which is acquired afresh with every generation'. Ever since English was used in Hong Kong, it has been adapted to the new local context by its indigenous users so that new forms and structures have been developed in phonetics and phonology, in the lexicon and in syntax,[1] which are, arguably, transmitted informally from one generation of HKE speakers to another. There are some sporadic studies exploring the phonetic/phonological aspects of this variety of English (e.g. Hung 2000;

---

[1] See Bolton (2000) for a guide to published research relevant to the study of HKE and Wong (2012) for an overview of major morphosyntactic features of HKE.

Peng and Ann 2004; Stibbard 2004; Setter 2006; Lim 2009), as well as its lexicon (e.g. Benson 1994, 2000; Carless 1995; Evans 2015; Wolf and Chan 2016). However, the grammatical description of HKE has been hitherto under-represented. Notable exceptions are Budge (1989) on the variable marking of plurals; Gisborne (2000) and Suárez-Gómez (2014) on the distinctive patterning of relative clauses; Lee (2001, 2004) on the usage and functions of modal verbs; Noël and Van der Auwera (2015) on a quantitative analysis of changes in the use of modals and quasi-modals in newspaper texts; Wong (2007, 2009) on tag questions and collective nouns; Yao (2016) on cleft constructions. These linguistic changes at different levels of description can be subsumed under the notion of 'structural nativisation' that is, 'the emergence of locally characteristic patterns and thus the genesis of a new variety of English' (Schneider 2007, pp. 5–6). As local norms have emerged and are now increasingly accepted as part of a localised variety of English, present-day HKE can be viewed as being nativised (see, for example, Setter et al. 2010; Evans 2011).

1.2   Sociocultural Background

Hong Kong is basically a monoethnic society with over 95 % of its total population being Chinese. In this regard, Chinese (in particular, Cantonese) is considered in this chapter as the dominant and substrate language whereas English is a non-dominant language. Despite being the non-dominant language, English has always held an official and very important position in Hong Kong. While Cantonese is spoken as the usual language by the majority (89.5 %) of the population (Census & Statistics Department 2011),[2] and has long been viewed as the language of solidarity and community ties (Cheung 1985; Lai 2009), English is seen as the language of success leading to higher education and better career prospects (Joseph 1996, 1997; Evans 2009). It is also valued as a global language and thus if Hong Kong is to gain a firm foothold in the

---

[2] Table A111 of the 2011 Population Census, 'Proportion of Population Aged 5 and Over Able to Speak Selected Languages/Dialects, 2001, 2006 and 2011', available at http://www.census2011.gov.hk/en/main-table/A111.html (accessed 14 June 2016).

international economy, good English skills in its workforce are considered to be essential. Given these circumstances, the Hong Kong government continues to stress the importance of English in its language policy for education after the return of Hong Kong to China, as evidenced in the compulsory benchmarking of all English language teachers (Qian 2008).

A detailed account of the language situation in Hong Kong has been given in Bolton (2000; 2003, pp. 93–99). Under British rule, the English language was 'the official language of government, the official language of law, and was *de facto* the more widely used medium of secondary and university education' (Bolton 2003, p. 93). It is not until 1995 that the Hong Kong government adopted a new language policy, which aimed to make its civil servants 'biliterate' in both English and Chinese and 'trilingual' in English, Cantonese and Putonghua (Lau 1995, p. 19). While this policy seems to give due emphasis to the Chinese language (both spoken and written forms), probably as a result of the 1997 handover to Chinese sovereignty, it has had a huge impact on the medium of instruction in primary and secondary schools in the territory. Throughout the 1980s and early 1990s, the government allowed individual schools to decide the teaching medium, leading to an increase in the proportion of 'Anglo-Chinese' schools, schools that advertised themselves as English-medium institutions and in fact did not provide a total immersion in an English-based education (Johnson 1994, p. 187). In those schools, Cantonese was used to teach almost all subjects but the majority of textbooks were in English and students took English-medium examinations. However, in a bid to promote the use of Chinese in the run-up to the handover, the government announced that in future around 100 secondary schools (some 22 %) would be allowed to use English as the medium of instruction (Kwok 1997).

One of the results of this language policy change is that the majority of schools are now using both spoken Cantonese and English (together with both Chinese and English textbooks) in a 'mixed mode' practice of teaching. Not only does it give rise to the emergence of 'Hong Kong English' (Mundy 1978; Strevens 1980; Todd and Hancock 1986; McArthur 1987, 2002), it also sets the scene for researching into notable structural features of this newly emerging variety of English, which is likely to be influenced by the substrate language, Cantonese. Furthermore, the use of English is increasingly common in certain socially conditioned contexts from the 1980s and

1990s onwards. There are a large number of Filipino domestic helpers in Hong Kong, who speak English to their employers, which makes it necessary to use English in the home. In fact, as cited in Gisborne (2009, p. 154), the 2006 Population By-Census (Census & Statistics Department 2006) shows that the percentage of the population claiming to speak English as either their usual language or as an additional language rose from 38.1 % in 1996, to 43 % in 2001, to 44.7 % in 2006. The figure has further risen to 46.1 % in the 2011 Population Census.[3] When it comes to English proficiency, the latest government survey suggests that in 2012 over 60 % of the population claimed to have 'very good', 'good' or 'average' competence in spoken English (Census & Statistics Department 2014). Now that English is increasingly in contact with the languages of the indigenous populations in domestic environments, it appears true enough to suggest that HKE is a variety with its own norms and its own local speech community.

1.3   Positioning the Book with Two Previously Published Monographs on HKE

The first ever monograph about HKE is Professor Kingsley Bolton's (2002) edited collection of scholarly articles addressing a wide spectrum of topics ranging from the sociolinguistic issues and distinctive linguistic features to the largely unnoticed creativity of literary texts. The significance of this first book is that it brings to the attention of the importance of recognising the newly emerging 'nativised' status of HKE to most of the people in the territory.

About a decade later, Setter et al. (2010) provide an up-to-date survey of current use of the variety. The book describes HKE as a linguistic phenomenon from the perspective of language structure and historical, sociocultural and sociopolitical development. While their book appears to be an invaluable contribution, it adopts a rather broad approach to the study of the variety. As stated in the blurb, it aims to 'provide an overview

---

[3] Table A111 of the 2011 Population Census, 'Proportion of Population Aged 5 and Over Able to Speak Selected Languages/Dialects, 2001, 2006 and 2011', available at http://www.census2011. gov.hk/en/main-table/A111.html (accessed 14 June 2016).

of all aspects of HKE in a style designed for undergraduates and general readers'. Very differently in terms of purpose and scope, what I hope to accomplish in this monograph is to provide in-depth case studies of a specific linguistic feature that is of significant importance to HKE with the target audience of graduate students and fellow researchers in the areas of World Englishes and Corpus Linguistics. As will be outlined shortly in the following chapter, although the issue of tag questions has been addressed in both Setter et al. (2010) and the current monograph, the former gives a two-page description of the feature whereas this book devotes a whole chapter to the subject. Aside from this contrast, the obvious point of departure consists in the kind of data used for analysis. This book is among one of the first few attempts (e.g. Bolton and Nelson 2002) to study HKE based on naturally occurring corpus data (both spoken and written) in the International Corpus of English (see the next section), while other studies either use invented or anecdotal examples or transcribed spoken data gathered from laboratory settings such as the map tasks employed by Setter et al. (2010). As Groves (2012) points out, the issue of representativeness is always taken for granted in previous studies of English in Hong Kong; she states that 'both the speakers and their speech samples chosen must be representative of the variety they speak, as this will affect the outcome of the research' (Groves 2012, p. 29). To ensure that research data is truly representative of any particular new English variety she suggests using the International Corpus of English, which 'already includes a wide range of text-types and proficiency levels' and 'avoids problematic issues such as how to get naturally occurring data' (Groves 2012, p. 42). Therefore, the Hong Kong component of the International Corpus of English, which will be outlined in the next section, represents a major step forward in the research of Hong Kong English.

1.4   The International Corpus of English (The Hong Kong Component) (ICE-HK)

In this book, I used the Hong Kong component of the International Corpus of English (ICE-HK), which was made publicly available in March 2006 (Nelson 2006a). The ICE-HK project was initiated in the

Table 1.1 Composition of the spoken ICE-HK

Dialogue	Monologue
S1A (413,287 words): Private (direct conversations and telephone calls)	S2A (126,857 words): Unscripted (spontaneous commentaries, unscripted speeches, demonstrations, legal presentations)
S1B (255,286 words): Public (class lessons, broadcast discussions, broadcast interviews, parliamentary debates, legal cross-examinations, business transactions)	S2B (119,793 words): Scripted (broadcast news, broadcast talks, non-broadcast talks)

early 1990s (Bolt and Bolton 1996). The ICE-HK corpus follows the common design of other ICE corpora worldwide, containing approximately 1 million words and including both spoken and written data using a ratio of 1.5:1 (Nelson 2006b, pp. 736–737; see also Nelson 1996). Tables 1.1 and 1.2 summarise the compositions of the spoken and written ICE-HK respectively.[4]

Bolton and Nelson's (2002) account pioneered the analysis of segments from the ICE-HK corpus for studying linguistic features of HKE. Certain linguistic features, vis-à-vis, the suprasegmentals of the Hong Kong accent, the noun phrase structure, phrasal verbs and coordination are highlighted as potential research areas. In its present form as a part-of-speech tagged corpus, ICE-HK does allow for partial interrogation of these features and provides a promising avenue for more sophisticated investigation alongside other levels of annotation such as syntactic and prosodic annotation (see McEnery et al. 2006, pp. 33–43 for the state-of-the-art description of these annotation types). Hence, the corpus is as a long-awaited, wide-ranging resource for empirical research into HKE, particularly in the context of lexicogrammatical and discoursal features, which this book seeks to explore at length.

In 2013 Professor Mark Davies of Brigham Young University created and released the Corpus of Global Web-based English (GloWbE). The GloWbE (Davies 2013; Davies and Fuchs 2015) is composed of 1.9 million words from 1.8 million web pages from 340,000 websites in

---

[4] See Wong (2010) for a full description of the composition of the ICE-HK corpus.

Table 1.2 Composition of the written ICE-HK

Non-printed	Printed
W1A (54,195 words): Non-professional writing (student essays and examination scripts)	W2A (118,717 words): Academic writing (Humanities, social sciences, natural sciences and technology)
W1B (79,768 words): Correspondence (social letters and business letters)	W2B (110,951 words): Non-academic writing (Humanities, social sciences, natural sciences and technology)
	W2C (51,589 words): Reportage (Press news reports)
	W2D (53,020 words): Instructional writing (administrative writing and skills and hobbies)
	W2E (24,561 words): Persuasive writing (press editorials)
	W2F (53,531 words): Creative writing (novels and stories)

20 different countries such as, the United States, Canada, Great Britain, Australia, India, Singapore, Philippines, Hong Kong, South Africa, Jamaica.[5] Specifically, the Hong Kong section of the GloWbE corpus totals approximately 40 million words. At first glance, GloWbE seems to perfectly complement the ICE-HK corpus data since it follows the same approach as in all ICE corpora with a roughly 60/40 mix of informal and more formal language, it also provides a web-based genre, which is missing in the sampling frame of the ICE-HK corpora that were largely built in the 1990s before the worldwide web. Nevertheless, as valuable as the GloWbE corpus is, one important limitation is that the linguistic identity of the author, who wrote the web pages, is completely unknown apart from the fact that the web pages are supposed to come from the country/ city in which a certain variety of English is being used (Nelson, 2015). The web pages (including blogs) were collected in December 2012 by running hundreds of high frequency multiword units against Google to generate random web pages, which were limited by country using Google's 'advanced search (region)' function. While it claims on the

---

[5] Efforts were made to remove duplicate texts, resulting in about 2 million unique web pages. For a full list of the twenty different countries and the size of the subcorpus for each of these countries, see http://corpus.byu.edu/glowbe/ (accessed 14 June 2016).

GloWbE web site that care has been taken to make sure that the IP address (which shows where the computer is physically located) indicates that about 95 % of the visitors to the site come from Hong Kong, and that 93 % of the links to that page are also from Hong Kong, it does not necessarily guarantee that the writer of the web page or blog is actually a person born and bred in Hong Kong whose English is being recorded; it might be someone who happened to reside in the city at the time of data collection. As Davies and Fuchs (2015, p. 26) admit, 'in GloWbE we only know that a website is from a particular country, but there might be speakers from other countries who have posted to that website. In ICE, on the other hand, care has been taken to ensure that all speakers are from the country in question.' With this consideration the GloWbE corpus has not been used in the present study. However, this is not to underestimate the range of possibilities for research with the corpus. It would definitely be useful for research studies particularly targeting web-based communication that characterise the range of new varietal features in non-Anglo English contexts in comparision to standard varieties of English such as British/American English: for example, Ooi et al. (2007) and Ooi and Tan (2014) undertook a sophisticated analysis of the systematicity of linguistic repertories used in personal webblogs and Facebook status updates and comments in Singapore(an) English. As Davies and Fuchs (2015, p. 5) note, '[a]s a result of the sampling process, all subcorpora [in GloWbE] constitute representative samples of how these national varieties of English are used in web-based communication.' Recognising the need to provide an analysis of web-based genres, which are not included in ICE-HK, Chap. 6 of this book will be devoted to studying the linguistic variation in the genre of blogs in Hong Kong English.

Based on data from the ICE Hong Kong corpus, then, an overview of the morphosyntactic features of HKE will be provided in the next section.

1.5   The Profile of Hong Kong English

The discussion of the morphosyntactic features of HKE revolves round three major areas, namely (1) features relating to pronouns and nouns; (2) features relating to tense (with particular reference to the present perfect); (3) features relating to redundant grammatical elements. This discussion includes a description of the features and a comparison with the substrate language (Cantonese).[6] It draws on data from the Hong Kong component of the International Corpus of English in order to base the analysis on most representative and objective evidence.

1.5.1 Features Relating to Pronouns and Nouns

Given that the Cantonese pronoun system is simpler than that of English (see, for example, Matthews and Yip 1994, pp. 79–84), it does not come as a surprise that HKE speakers tend to remove some distinctions that are made in standard varieties of English. First, the pronouns in Cantonese have a single form for subject or object. This is in contrast to the English pronouns that have different forms in subject and object positions (e.g. *I* (subject) vs. *me* (object)). This distinction does not hold in HKE, however. Examples (1)–(3) clearly illustrate that HKE speakers use *me* instead of *I* in coordinate subjects.

Using me instead of I in coordinate subjects

(1) <ICE-HK:S1A-058#1062–3:1:A> Because *me and your mom* <.> Or </.> Often go <.> sh </.> shopping together.[7]

(2) <ICE-HK:S2A-033#136:1:A> I think it's something that is simple and is very clearly delineated that the public can understand and more importantly that *me and my colleagues* can understand and can take part in.

(3) <ICE-HK:S1A-035#X463:1:Z> So actually *me and my family* we don't get involved in politics so we don't really care about what's happening in politics you know so whatever happens we just lead our own life and we just do our own thing

Second, as there is no gender distinction between *he*, *she* and *it* in Cantonese (i.e. the same form *keoi5* is used for the third person singular),

---

[6] Transcriptions of Cantonese in this chapter follow the Linguistic Society of Hong Kong (1997).

[7] The <.> tag indicates incomplete words in the original recordings (Nelson, 2006a, p. 6).

HKE speakers find it difficult to uphold this distinction. As in examples (4)–(9), the deliberate self-repair—from she to he and from he to she, is telling. While HKE is actively undergoing the process of structural nativisation (see Sect. 1.1) to become a variety of English in its own right, with a distinct indigenous vocabulary and the emergence and positive attitude towards code-mixing (Schneider 2007, pp. 138–139), there are still traces of 'exonormative stablisation' in which the language of the colonial community is considered as a role model of language standards and norms (Schneider 2007, p. 32). In the examples, there seems to be confusion over the gender of the third person singular pronoun because, on the one hand, the Cantonese substrate does not have this gender distinction, but on the other hand, the need (if any) for orientation towards standard English (StE) norms felt by these HKE speakers have prompted the use of the 'correct' gender in the third-person singular pronoun.

Confusion over gender distinction in third person singular (deliberate self-repair from *she* to *he*)

(4) <ICE-HK:S1A-054#X49–52:1:Z> Just now *one son* has returned to work here. Uhm. Uh. Oh, *she uh he* also like to work in Hong Kong.

(5) <ICE-HK:S1A-037#319–20:1:A> But once *he* uhm *he* uhm when *he* one in a time *he* uh went to Taiwan for a tourist tour- tourism. And for three two or three months and then *oh she uh he his* <.> Pu </.> *his* Mandarin is very good after he back to Hong Kong

(6) <ICE-HK:S1A-023#X336:1:Z> Yeah <?> isn't it <?> and *she he* is the only *male* </X>[8]

(deliberate self-repair from *he* to *she*)

(7) <ICE-HK:S1B-002#210–1:1:A> Okay now it is a *Ruth* is a very good woman. And *he is she is* so good that she's willing to look after her mother-in-law

(8) <ICE-HK:S1A-052#X549:1:Z> *His sister* is in uh

---

[8] The <?> element marks the transcription as unclear and uncertain (Nelson, 2006a, p. 6).

<ICE-HK:S1A-052#550:1:A> Singapore
<ICE-HK:S1A-052#X551–5:1:Z> Stafford. No. In UK. Birmingham. You know Birmingham
<ICE-HK:S1A-052#556:1:A> In fact no
<ICE-HK:S1A-052#X557:1:Z> *He's she's* in Staffordshire

(9) <ICE-HK:S1A-001#430:1:A> Yeah but but actually uhm even even in the new Lunar New Year I have visited *her* but actually *he she* really is not not really want to see me actually so uhm

Apparently, gender distinction for pronouns in third person singular poses particular problems for HKE speakers. The fact that there is no number distinction in reflexive pronouns is another important issue. The reflexive pronoun *ourselves* is spoken as *ourself* in HKE, as can be seen in examples (10) and (11).

No number distinction in reflexives i.e. plural forms ending in -self

(10) <ICE-HK:S1A-080#11:1:B> Uh but I'm afraid that uh we go uhm to Europe by *ourself* just two girls it will it will be too dangerous

(11) <ICE-HK:S1A-061#1123–6:1:A> How can you skip this system
<ICE-HK:S1A-061#X1124:1:Z> Not *ourself.* Because it didn't occur during my time. You understand.

Specifically, the plural form *-selves* becomes the singular *-self* in HKE. While standard varieties of English have a distinction between singular and plural reflexive pronouns, HKE speakers do not, partly because that there is no such distinction in Cantonese. The ending *-self* in English corresponds to *zi6gei2* in Cantonese, which is invariable in form for both singular and plural reflexive pronouns (Matthews and Yip 1994, p. 84). The number distinction is in fact marked by the preceding personal pronoun used together with *zi6gei2* (i.e. *ngo5 zi6gei2* 'myself' vs. *ngo5dei6 zi6gei2* 'ourselves').[9] As the reflexive pronoun *zi6gei2* makes no number distinction in Cantonese, HKE speakers tend to carry

---

[9] The suffix *-dei6* indicates plurality in Cantonese.

over this feature in their speaking English resulting in plural reflexive forms ending in -*self*.

The breakdown of count/mass noun distinctions in HKE can also be traced back to the syntax of the substrate. The overall structure of a noun phrase in Cantonese is similar to English, with the difference that a classifier (CL) is required in the former but not in the latter. Hence, the order of the elements of the noun phrase in Cantonese is as follows: demonstrative, numeral, classifier, adjective, noun. As Matthews and Yip (1994, p. 92) point out, the major functions of classifiers are in counting or enumerating, as in *loeng5 zek3 daan2* two CL egg 'two eggs', as well as in individuating nouns, as in *ni1 zek3 daan2* this CL egg 'this egg'. These functions of the classifiers give rise to two types of classifier: (1) measure classifiers, e.g. *di1*, denote plurality or uncountable substances; (2) type classifiers, e.g. *go3, zek3*, reflect intrinsic features of the nouns with which they belong. Essentially, the mass/count distinction resides in the noun classifiers in Cantonese. While measure classifiers can be used to denote both count and mass nouns (e.g. *di1 jan4* CL person 'the/some people' vs. *di1 seoi2* CL water 'the/some water'), type classifiers can be used to denote count nouns only (e.g. *ni1 go3 jan4* this CL person 'this person').

Now let us return to the issue of the absence of count/mass noun distinctions in HKE with reference to the noun phrase structure in Cantonese. On the one hand, the absence of a noun classifier in English would mean that the mass/count distinction would be easily lost with HKE speakers whose substrate system basically employs a classifier to make that distinction, with measure classifiers for both count and mass nouns and type classifiers for count nouns only. On the other hand, the mass/count distinction appears to be neutralised as the same measure classifier can be used, like English *some*, to denote a quantity of either countable things or uncountable substances, as in *gei2 faan1 syut3waa6* some CL words 'these words as a whole' vs. *gei2 faan1 zung1guk1* some CL advice 'this advice as a whole'. The mass/count distinction in Cantonese is therefore not as clear cut as in English. The combined effect of these two facts—(1) the absence of a noun classifier in English and (2) the use of an identical measure classifier for both count and mass nouns— results in the easy loss of the mass/count distinction in HKE. As shown in the following examples, the mass/count distinction is lost and thus HKE speakers attach the plural marker -s/-es to the end of what is apparently a mass noun in standard varieties of English. These examples are largely in line with the findings of an earlier study; Joseph (2004, pp. 144–147) suggests a lack of the mass/count distinction in HKE noun phrases, for example, *a bowl of noodle*, on the basis of partial structural transfer from Chinese.

No count/mass noun distinctions resulting in use of plural for StE singular

(12) <ICE-HK:S1A-079#323:1:C> The *staffs* are nice

(13) <ICE-HK:S2A-058#75:1:A> When people hear interior design some people think oh what's it got to do with *furnitures* right

(14) <ICE-HK:W1B-014#9:1> What are your *advices*?

(15) <ICE-HK:W1A-004#61:1> Children like to pay attention and imitate the *behaviours* of other, adult is the model that they to imitate.

(16) <ICE-HK:W1B-004#14:1> Except it is made in Korea, all the materials and *equipments* are come from USA.

(17) <ICE-HK:S1A-063#461:1:A> Besides the stable that is a resort called Sai Laih Wuh <&> resort-in-China </&> resort where they have all kind of uh *entertainments* and games there like uhm[10]

(18) <ICE-HK:S2A-047#46:1:A> And uh I'll give you some supporting *evidences* in a <.> min </.> in a minute

(19) <ICE-HK:S1A-093#85:1:B> I have do a lot of *homeworks* to do

(20) <ICE-HK:S2A-024#25:1:A> Uhm now I would like to start the tour by telling you some general *informations* about Hong Kong okay

(21) <ICE-HK:W1A-009#59:1> All those *researches* have received the acceptance of the majority of organists, especially the English organists; perhaps because the consistent, steady and securely based on the research of their scholars.

(22) <ICE-HK:S1A-087#X497:1:Z> The written is mainly homework and that's just get the *vocabularies* right and the grammar right

---

[10] The <&> element includes editorial comment (Nelson, 2006a, p. 6).

1.5.2   Features Relating to Tense

As is well-known, there is no tense contrast in Chinese (see Hu et al. 2001 for a full set of arguments). Indeed in the *World Atlas of Language Structure* (Dahl and Velupillai 2008), Sinitic languages (e.g. Mandarin Chinese and Cantonese) are among those that do not distinguish between past and present, whereas English is among those languages that show a past/present contrast. This marked difference between Cantonese and English with regard to tense explains why tense contrasts are suspended in HKE, where a verb is clearly used with past time reference but appears in the base form of the verb. Gisborne (2000, cited in Gisborne 2009, pp. 160–161) gives the following examples, showing that HKE is non-tensed.

(23) In my first year, Cats come to Hong Kong.
(24) He is born in Hong Kong and then just go to Hong Kong.
(25) China want to took ... wants to take over.

Unsuprisingly, in McArthur's *Oxford Guide to World English* (2002) one of the features of HKE is that the present tense is commonly used for past and future events, for example, *I come here yesterday* (2002, p. 360). However, what has not been well-researched in relation to tense in HKE is the levelling of the difference between the present prefect and the past simple presented in examples (26) and (27).
   Levelling of the difference between present perfect and simple past: present perfect for StE simple past

(26) <ICE-HK:W1B-019#291:17> The concern of water quality of Wisdom Court *has been raised* by other residents <u>a few months ago</u>.
(27) <ICE-HK:S1A-021#X185:1:Z> He is also uhm he *has* also *migrated* to States from Singapore <u>about forty years ago</u> already

In Standard English (see, for example, Leech 2006, pp. 92–93), the present perfect tense refers to something taking place in a period leading up to the present moment. It competes with the past tense as both tenses are used to refer to past time. But the present prefect is distinguished from the past simple as it refers not only to the past but to the 'past with relevance to the present': while the present perfect is used to refer to an action/state of affairs that happened at an unspecified time before now (the moment of speaking), we use the past tense to indicate an action/state of affairs that happened at a definite time in the past and no longer exists now.

So this 'present relevance' is the key to understanding the difference between the two tenses. The 'key', however, is useless for HKE speakers whose substrate language does not have a past/present contrast as noted above. To make matters worse, the perfective aspect (of the present perfect tense) is realised by the same grammatical element in the substrate for the past simple—the perfective (PFV) particle (PRT) *zo2*. Not only can the particle *zo2* be used in reporting past events (corresponding to the simple past) as in example (28), but it can also be used to express a period of time up to and including the present (corresponding to the present perfect) as in example (29). Both of these examples are taken from Matthews and Yip (1994, p. 205).

(28)   *gung1si1*   *gau6lin2*   *zaan6zo2*   *m4siu2*   *cin2*
        company   last.year   earn-PFV   not.little   money
        'The company made a good deal of money last year'

(29)   *lei5dei6*   *git3-zo3-fan1*   *gei2*   *loi6*   *a3?*
        you-PL   marry-PFV   now   long   PRT
        'How long have you been married?'

Under the influence of the perfective aspect marker *zo2* from the substrate, HKE speakers are more likely to use the present perfect for past events that should be described using the past simple in standard varieties of English, as in examples (26) and (27) above.

The perfect marker *already* in HKE gives further evidence for this sort of substrate influence. In the absence of explicit tense marking, the expression of time is marked by a combination of adverbials, aspect markers and contextual factors in Cantonese (Matthews and Yip 1994,

p. 198). Again, this substrate feature plays a role in the way in which temporal relations are expressed in HKE; the dimension of time is usually specified by another word or phrase, typically an adverb(ial), as in examples (30)–(32) from the ICE-HK corpus.

(30) <ICE-HK:S1A-053#X61:1:Z> Actually John Ducan *call* me <u>this morning</u> to say that he's doing a section on Friday, about the new, CE oral

(31) <ICE-HK:S1A-034#X30:1:Z> So you both *miss* class <u>last week</u>

(32) <ICE-HK:S2B-004#4:1:A> Ambassador <?> Ma Yiu Jeng </?> *arrives* <u>tomorrow</u> for a brief stay before traveling to Beijing

Similarly, in HKE the adverb *already* is often used to refer to events that happened at an indefinite time in the past with continuation or effects up to the present, like the English perfect (cf. Werner 2013, pp. 216–221). Examples of *already* as a perfect marker can be found in ICE-HK.

Perfect marker *already*

(33) <ICE-HK:S2B-029#66:1:A> We *already* had our first meeting with representatives of ten professional bodies to make out our action plan

(34) <ICE-HK:W1B-024#222:14> Further to our fax message to you yesterday, we *already* received confirmation of survey agent agreeing to handle this case and report to us.

(35) <ICE-HK:W1B-020#31:2> Pls find attached the invoice for the said shipment for you to arrange the T/T payment, as I *already* obtained the MATE RECEIPT, and since the ship *already* left Hong Kong today, therefore, I can take the mate receipt to PIFF tomorrow for changing the Bills of Lading, then maybe I can even fax the said document to you by tomorrow late afternoon, and send you the original copy by Thursday morning.

1.5.3 Features Relating to Redundant Grammatical Elements

So far we have seen cases where features of the standard varieties of English are either not realised (Sect. 1.5.1) or are mixed up (Sect. 1.5.2) in HKE. In this section, we will consider examples in which some grammatical elements are used by HKE speakers that are considered redundant in Standard English.

First, to link two clauses, HKE speakers use two conjunctions (see examples (36)–(39)) whereas in standard varieties of English, if the first clause begins with *although* or *since*, the second clause cannot begin with *but* or *so*. This is a perfect illustration of morphosyntactic transfer from Cantonese in which clauses are joined by correlative (or paired) conjunctions.

Conjunction doubling: correlative conjuctions

(36) <ICE-HK:S2A-023#136:7:A> *Although* they are not uh very much *but* at least there are some differences

(37) <ICE-HK:W1B-014#11:1> *Although* I have gone to the spectacle shop to buy contact lenses *but* I have not got the contact lenses yet.

(38) <ICE-HK:S1A-004#X483:1:Z> *Since* you're both the eldest *so* you can complain about your younger sister and your younger brother <&> all laughed </&> right

(39) <ICE-HK:W1B-016#356:15> *Since* this section runs worldwide anyway, *so* there is only one cost to your insertions.

Secondly, in the ICE-HK data, some causative verbs such as *make* and *let* select for *to*-infinitive clausal complements whereas Standard English has bare infinitives.

Addition of to where StE has bare infinitive

(40) <ICE-HK:S1A-012#X82:1:Z> Uh I think we'll <?> be </?> they make you *to* uhm *to* take lot of test like English test and those kind of numerical test

(41) <ICE-HK:S1A-062#350:1:A> So how can you uh even if you if you're girl how can you uh make them *to* go away

(42) <ICE-HK:S2B-024#132:3:A> I understand that it will take time to let Chinese official *to* see why and how did Chinese style upset Hong Kong peoples time and again

(43) <ICE-HK:S2A-060#205:1:A> Some of them they even don't let other people *to* read it within three years within two years or never want anybody to read his <.> the </.> he his or her thesis okay

(44) <ICE-HK:S1A-022#185:1:A> Just let the Chinese oh no just let the Hong Kong elite *to* rule Hong Kong

This finding is surprising as the bare infinitive seems a much more reasonable choice due to substrate transfer. Cantonese has been well-known for its serial verb (V_1–V_2) constructions (Matthews 2006, p. 69). A parallel structure to English causative verbs is therefore a causative serial construction (see the following Cantonese examples taken from Matthews 2006, p. 75).

(45)

ngo5	zing2	keoi5	dit3
I	make	3sg	fall

'I made him fall'

(46)

lei5	jiu3	tam3	keoi5	hoi1sam1
you	need	pacify	3sg	happy

'You need to make her happy'

As Matthews (2006, p. 75) points out, these causative verbs V_1 and V_2 (underlined)[11] 'all exist as main verbs in their own right', contrary to the fact that in English V_2 has to be non-finite. Hence, the redundant use of *to* in the HKE examples appears to be an overgeneralisation of a typologically marked (or salient) feature in English in that verbs require a finite clausal complement in English whereas the substrate language Cantonese

---

[11] In Cantonese the categorical distinction between adjectives and verbs is hard to establish and thus V_2 in example (46) can be a stative verb or an adjective, both of which can function as predicate.

does not have this feature. This over-generalisation has also been extended to other verbs such as *suggest* in HKE. In a search of ICE-HK, there were several tokens of *suggest* with non-finite complement clauses, that is, failing to make the mood or modality contrast that is required in normal uses of *suggest*.

(47) <ICE-HK:S1A-085#69:1:A> They think that English is too hard for them so I suggest them *to* change to uh an Chinese uh <indig> ngh haih </indig> an <.> s </.> secondary school taught by Chinese but their mother uh dislike dislike uh secondary school talk by Chinese[12]

(48) <ICE-HK:S1B-075#X237:1:Z> You select the fund by yourself or the Hong Kong Bank suggest you *to* select this

(49) <ICE-HK:W1B-021#182:8> I may suggest you *to* stay with our main hotel for the first two nights so as to enjoy this special offer and then change back to Towers for the rest of your stay if you don't mind of moving.

Indeed, recognising that the feature system of English is topologically marked relative to Cantonese allows us to bring the use of *to* following *make*, *let* and *suggest* phenomenon under the same generalisation. From a typological and evolutionary perspective, English and Cantonese are contact languages, generating a pool of linguistically diverse features (Ansaldo 2009). In this feature pool approach features that are salient in the pool will surface in the contact grammar, which has been argued here as HKE. The sociolinguistics of Hong Kong (see Sect. 1.2) indicate that the most frequently found morphosyntactic features in the pool are those of Cantonese so it is unsurprising that Cantonese morphosyntax transfers into HKE (see Sects. 1.5.1 and 1.5.2). However, we do not only allow for the possibility of substrate transfer, but we also expect that when superstrate features are very salient they can make their way into HKE, as with the case of the overgeneralisation of *to*-infinitives (a salient feature in English) with *make*, *let* and *suggest* as outlined above.

---

[12] The <indig> element encloses an indigenous expression (Nelson, 2006a, p. 6).

1.6 Concluding Remarks and Structure of the Book

This introductory chapter has set out some of the essential information needed to begin a corpus-based study of Hong Kong English, and sketched a brief depiction of the empirical exploration of HKE in terms of various linguistic features. Also in this chapter, we have looked at some data that shows that some speakers of HKE have a grammar system that is typologically similar to Cantonese. It has been argued that the kinds of levelling of morphosyntactic distinctions that are common in HKE can be accounted for by the relevant substrate structures. But there is a complication: the self-correction of third-person singular pronouns and the over-generalised selection by some causative verbs (i.e. *make* and *let*) of a finite complement tend to be robust evidence for the (imperfect) transfer of the grammar of Standard English to speakers of HKE. It appears then that the system transfers from the substrate do not serve as absolute proof that what has happened here is that Hong Kong people have developed their own English. As Jenkins (2009, p. 151) puts it, 'the status of HKE is still ambivalent.' What we see is an emerging system with a considerable degree of variability, with HKE at stage 3 (i.e. as a nativising variety) in Schneider's (2007) dynamic model.

But the most important conclusion is the importance of studying 'angloversal' features of a range of diverse kinds.[13] The typological approach allows us to establish a fine grained lexicogrammatical description of the relevant features of an emerging variety of English such as HKE. Hence, this book will provide a thorough explanation of the research findings based on influences from the substrate language Cantonese. As noted above, in Hong Kong's colonial past, the presence of English led to a situation of language contact, in which the substrate language interacted with the superstrate language. As a consequence, a new linguistic variety, HKE, emerged in the territory. In this process of language contact, the great influence of the local language at all linguistic levels is taken for granted (Mesthrie 2004, p. 808); this is particularly clear

---

[13] As, for example, Kortmann and Szmrecsanyi (2004) argue.

in the case of lexis, which represents the local linguistic ecology, and also in grammar and discourse/pragmatics. This book is thus aims to address the existing gap in the scholarship where substrate influences have largely been ignored.

The following chapters will each focus on a specific linguistic feature that has yet to be studied, providing detailed case studies of the different aspects of this variety of English. It is important to study key areas of lexicogrammar and discourse because as Schneider (2007, p. 46) explains, the most telling sign of the birth of a new, formally distinct English variety tends to occur at the interface between grammar and lexis, 'affecting the syntactic behaviour of certain lexical elements. Individual words, typically high-frequency items, adopt characteristic but marked usage and complementation patterns', thereby developing constructions peculiar to the respective variety.

The rest of the book is structured in the following way. In Part I: Lexicogrammar, the localised features of HKE and their substrate influences at the levels of lexis and grammar will be considered. Chapter 2 looks at issues to do with tag questions in order to address questions such as how participation of interlocutors can be encouraged by a certain polarity type of tag constructions. Chapter 3 considers collective nouns and how semantic/pragmatic motivation plays a crucial role in concord patterns with these nouns. In Part II: Discourse, Chap. 4 investigates how the corpus approach can be employed in order to examine linguistic phenomena that occur beyond the sentence level, by looking at expressions of gratitude in extended discourse, whereas Chap. 5 is concerned with code-mixing whereby indigenous Cantonese words are occasionally incorporated into English discourse as a potential marker of ethnic identity for the Hong Kong speakers of English. Chapter 6 looks at the blog variety of digital discourse in HKE as compared to British English based on GloWbE. Chapter 7 concludes the book with a summary of major corpus findings and a discussion of the emergent issues. It also re-addresses some of the concerns that have been raised in this introduction about the status of HKE as an emerging nativised variety of English.

References

Ansaldo, Umberto. 2009. The Asian Typology of English: Theoretical and Methodological Considerations. *English World-Wide* 30(2): 133–148.

Benson, Phil. 1994. The Political Vocabulary in Hong Kong English. *Hong Kong Papers in Linguistics and Language Teaching* 17(1): 63–81.

———. 2000. Hong Kong Words: Variation and Context. *World Englishes* 19 (3): 373–380.

Bolt, Philip, and Kingsley Bolton. 1996. The International Corpus of English in Hong Kong. In *Comparing English Worldwide: The International Corpus of English*, ed. Sidney Greenbaum, 197–214. Oxford: Clarendon Press.

Bolton, Kingsley. 2000. Researching Hong Kong English: Bibliographical Resources. *World Englishes* 19(3): 445–452.

———., ed. 2002. *Hong Kong English: Autonomy and Creativity*. Hong Kong: Hong Kong University Press.

———. 2003. *Chinese Englishes: A Sociolinguistic History*. Cambridge: Cambridge University Press.

Bolton, Kingsley, and Gerald Nelson. 2002. Analysing Hong Kong English: Sample Texts from the International Corpus of English. In *Hong Kong English: Autonomy and Creativity*, ed. Kingsley Bolton, 241–264. Hong Kong: Hong Kong University Press.

Budge, Carol. 1989. Plural Marking in Hong Kong English. *HongKong Papers in Linguistics and Language Teaching* 12(1989): 39–47.

Carless, David. 1995. Politicised Expressions in the South China Morning Post. *English Today* 11(2): 18–22.

Census & Statistics Department. 2006. Population By-Census. http://www.bycensus2006.gov.hk/en/index.htm. Accessed 14 June 2016.

———. 2011. Population Census. http://www.census2011.gov.hk/en/index.html. Accessed 14 June 2016.

———. 2014. Hong Kong Monthly Digest of Statistics: June 2014 Feature Article: Use of Language in Hong Kong in 2012. http://www.statistics.gov.hk/pub/B71406FB2014XXXXB0100.pdf Accessed 7 July 2016.

Cheung, Yat-shing. 1985. Power, Solidarity and Luxury in Hong Kong: A Sociolinguistic Study. *Anthropological Linguistics* 27(2): 190–203.

Dahl, Östen, and Viveka Velupillai. 2008. The Past Tense. In *The World Atlas of Language Structures Online*, ed. Martin Haspelmath, Matthew S. Dryer, David Gil, and Bernard Comrie, 66. Munich: Max Planck Digital Library. http://wals.info/feature/66. Accessed 14 June 2016.

Davies, Mark. 2013. Corpus of Global Web-Based English: 1.9 Billion Words from Speakers in 20 Countries. http://corpus.byu.edu/glowbe/. Accessed 14 June 2016.

Davies, Mark, and Robert Fuchs. 2015. Expanding Horizons in the Study of World Englishes with the 1.9 Billion Word Global Web-Based English Corpus (GloWbE). *English World-Wide* 36(1): 1–28.

Evans, Stephen. 2009. The Evolution of the English-Language Speech Community in Hong Kong. *English World-Wide* 30(3): 278–301.

———. 2011. Hong Kong English: The Growing Pains of a New Variety. *Asian Englishes* 14(1): 22–45.

———. 2015. Testing the Dynamic Model: The Evolution of the Hong Kong English Lexicon (1858–2012). *Journal of English Linguistics* 43(3): 175–200.

Gisborne, Nikolas. 2000. Relative Clauses in Hong Kong English. *World Englishes* 19(3): 357–371.

———. 2009. Aspects of the Morphosyntactic Typology of Hong Kong English. *English World-Wide* 30(2): 149–169.

Groves, Julie. 2012. The Issue of Representativeness in Hong Kong English. *Asian Englishes* 15(1): 28–45.

Hu, Jianhua, Haihua Pan, and Liejiong Xu. 2001. Is There a Finite vs. - Non-Finite Distinction in Chinese? *Linguistics* 39(6): 1117–1148.

Hung, Tony. 2000. Towards a Phonology of Hong Kong English. *World Englishes* 19(3): 337–356.

Jenkins, Jennifer. 2009. *World Englishes: A Resource Book for Students*. 2nd ed. London and New York: Routledge.

Johnson, Robert K. 1994. Language Policy and Planning in Hong Kong. *Annual Review of Applied Linguistics* 14(1): 177–199.

Joseph, John. 1996. English in Hong Kong: Emergence and Decline. *Current Issues in Language and Society* 3(2): 166–179.

———. 1997. English in Hong Kong: Emergence and Decline. In *One Country, Two Systems, Three Languages: A Survey of Changing Language Use in Hong Kong*, ed. Sue Wright and Helen Kelly-Holmes, 60–79. Cleveon: Multilingual Matters.

———. 2004. *Language and Identity: National, Ethnic, Religious*. Basingstoke: Palgrave Macmillan.

Kortmann, Bernd, and Benedikt Szmrecsanyi. 2004. Global Synopsis: Morphological and Syntactic Variation in English. In *A Handbook of Varieties of English*, Vol. 2: *Morphology and Syntax*, ed. Bernd Kortmann, Kate Burridge,

Rajend Mesthrie, Edgar W. Schneider, and Clive Upton, 1142–1202. Berlin and New York: Mouton de Gruyter.

Kwok, Shirley. 1997. New Rule Will Halve Schools Using English. *South China Morning Post*, 22 March, p. 7.

Lai, Mee-ling. 2009. 'I Love Cantonese, But I Want English'—A Qualitative Account of Hong Kong Students' Language Attitudes. *The Asia-Pacific Education Researchers* 18(1): 79–92.

Lau, Chi-kuen. 1995. Language of the Future. *South China Morning Post*, 18 September, p. 19.

Lee, Jackie. 2001. Functions of *Need* in Australian English and Hong Kong English. *World Englishes* 20(2): 133–143.

———. 2004. On the Usage of *Have, Dare, Need, Ought To* and *Used To* in Australian English and Hong Kong English. *World Englishes* 23(4): 501–513.

Leech, Geoffrey. 2006. *A Glossary of English Grammar*. Edinburgh: Edinburgh University Press.

Li, David C.S. 1999. The Functions and Status of English in Hong Kong: A Post-1997 Update. *English World-Wide* 20(1): 67–110.

Lim, Lisa. 2009. Revisiting Prosody: (Some) New Englishes as Tone Languages? *English World-Wide* 30(2): 218–239.

Linguistic Society of Hong Kong. 1997. *Jyut6 ping3* [Cantonese Romanisation Scheme]. Hong Kong: Linguistic Society of Hong Kong. (In Chinese).

Luke, Dan, and Jack Richards. 1982. English in Hong Kong: Functions and Status. *English World-Wide* 3(1): 47–64.

Matthews, Stephen. 2006. On Serial Verb Constructions in Cantonese. In *Serial Verbs: A Cross-Linguistic Typology*, ed. Alexandra Y. Aikhenvald and R.M.W. Dixon, 69–87. Oxford: Oxford University Press.

Matthews, Stephen, and Virginia Yip. 1994. *Cantonese: A Comprehensive Grammar*. London and New York: Routledge.

McArthur, Tom. 1987. The English Languages? *English Today* 3(3): 9–13.

———. 2002. *The Oxford Guide to World English*. Oxford and New York: Oxford University Press.

McEnery, Tony, Richard Xiao, and Tono Yukio. 2006. *Corpus-Based Language Studies: An Advanced Resource Book*. London and New York: Routledge.

Mesthrie, Rajend. 2004. Introduction: Varieties of English in Africa and South and Southeast Asia. In *A Handbook of Varieties of English*, Vol. 2: *Morphology and Syntax*, ed. Bernd Kortmann, Kate Burridge, Rajend Mesthrie, Edgar W. Schneider, and Clive Upton, 805–812. Berlin: Mouton de Gruyter.

Mundy, John. 1978. *Communicative Syllabus Design*. Cambridge: Cambridge University Press.

Nelson, Gerald. 1996. The Design of the Corpus. In *Comparing English Worldwide: The International Corpus of English*, ed. Sidney Greenbaum, 27–35. Oxford: Clarendon Press.

———. 2006a. *The ICE Hong Kong Corpus: User Manual*. London: University College London.

———. 2006b. World Englishes and Corpora Studies. In *The Handbook of World Englishes*, ed. Braj Kachru, Yamuna Kachru, and Cecil Nelson, 733–750. Malden, MA and Oxford: Blackwell.

———. 2015. Response to Mark Davies and Robert Fuchs, Expanding Horizons in the Study of World Englishes with the 1.9 Billion Word Global Web-Based English Corpus (GloWbE). *English World-Wide* 36(1): 38–40.

Noël, Dirk, and Johan Van der Auwera. 2015. Recent Quantitative Changes in the Use of Modals and Quasi-Modals in the Hong Kong, British and American Printed Press: Exploring the Potential of Factiva® for the Diachronic Investigation of World Englishes. In *Grammatical Change in English World-Wide*, ed. Peter Collins, 437–464. Amsterdam and Philadelphia: John Benjamins.

Ooi, Vincent B.Y., and Peter K.W. Tan. 2014. Facebook, Linguistic Identity and Hybridity in Singapore. In *The Global-Local Interface and Hybridity: Exploring Language and Identity*, ed. Rani Rubdy and Lubna Alsagoff, 225–244. Bristol, Buffalo and Toronto: Multilingual Matters.

Ooi, Vincent B.Y., Peter K.W. Tan, and Andy K.L. Chiang. 2007. Analysing Personal Weblogs in Singapore English: The WMatrix Approach. In *eVariEng* (Journal of the Research Unit for Variation, Contacts, and Change in English), Vol. 2: *Towards Multimedia in Corpus Studies*. Finland: University of Helsinki. http://www.helsinki.fi/varieng/series/volumes/02/ooi_et_al/. Accessed 14 June 2016.

Pang, Terence. 2003. Hong Kong English: A Stillborn Variety? *English Today* 19 (2): 12–18.

Peng, Long, and Jean Ann. 2004. Obstruent Voicing and Devoicing in the English of Cantonese Speakers from Hong Kong. *World Englishes* 23(4): 535–564.

Qian, David. 2008. English Language Assessment in Hong Kong: A Survey of Practices, Developments and Issues. *Language Testing* 25(1): 85–110.

Schneider, Edgar. 2007. *Postcolonial English: Varieties Around the World*. Cambridge: Cambridge University Press.

Setter, Jane. 2006. Speech Rhythm in World Englishes: The Case of Hong Kong. *TESOL Quarterly* 40(4): 763–782.

Setter, Jane, Cathy Wong, and Brian Chan. 2010. *Hong Kong English*. Edinburgh: Edinburgh University Press.

Stibbard, Richard. 2004. The Spoken English of Hong Kong: A Study of Co-Occurring Segmental Errors. *Language, Culture and Curriculum* 17(2): 127–142.

Strevens, Peter. 1980. *Teaching English as an International Language*. Oxford: Pergamon.

Suárez-Gómez, Cristina. 2014. Relative Clauses in Southeast Asian Englishes. *Journal of English Linguistics* 42(3): 245–268.

Todd, Loreto, and Ian Hancock. 1986. *International English Usage*. London: Groom Helm.

Tsui, Amy B.M., and David Bunton. 2000. The Discourse and Attitudes of English Language Teachers in Hong Kong. In *Hong Kong English: Autonomy and Creativity*, ed. Kingsley Bolton, 287–303. Hong Kong: Hong Kong University Press.

Werner, Valentin. 2013. Temporal Adverbials and the Present Perfect/Past Tense Alternation. *English World-Wide* 34(2): 202–240.

Wolf, Hans-Georg, and Thomas Chan. 2016. Understanding Asia by Means of Cognitive Sociolinguistics and Cultural Linguistics—The Example of GHOSTS in Hong Kong English. In *Communicating with Asia: The Future of English as a Global Language*, ed. Gerhard Leitner, Azirah Hashim, and Hans-Georg Wolf, 249–266. Cambridge: Cambridge University Press.

Wong, May L-Y. 2007. Tag Questions in Hong Kong English: A Corpus-Based Study. *Asian Englishes* 10(1): 44–61.

———. 2009. *Committee, Staff, Council*, etc.: A Corpus Analysis of Collective Nouns in Hong Kong English. *Asian Englishes* 12(1): 4–19.

———. 2010. Expressions of Gratitude by Hong Kong Speakers of English: Research from the Internationa7l Corpus of English in Hong Kong (ICE-HK). *Journal of Pragmatics* 42(5): 1243–1257.

———. 2012. Hong Kong English. In *The Mouton World Atlas of Variation in English*, ed. Bernd Kortmann and Kerstin Lunkenheimer, 548–561. Berlin and New York: Mouton de Gruyter.

Yao, Xinyue. 2016. Cleft Constructions in Hong Kong English. *English World-Wide* 37(2): 197–220.

Part I

Lexicogrammar

2

Tag Questions

Abstract Providing a quantitative and qualitative account of the use of tag questions in Hong Kong English (HKE), Wong analyses around 200 instances of question tags extracted from the ICE-HK corpus. She reveals that Hong Kong speakers of English tend to disproportionately use more positive-positive tag constructions (e.g. *It's pretty, is it?*) than native English speakers, with '*is it?*' being used as a universal question tag. Looking at the communicative functions of these tag questions, Wong demonstrates that Hong Kong people tend to use tags primarily for confirming and encouraging participation of speakers in conversation. The chapter also discusses possible cross-cultural implications of the tendencies of tag questions in HKE.

Keywords Tag questions • Polarity • Confirmation • Conversation • Hong Kong English

© The Author(s) 2017
M. Wong, *Hong Kong English*,
DOI 10.1057/978-1-137-51964-1_2

2.1   Introduction

Extensive attention has been given to tag questions in the literature. While a majority of these studies are qualitative in their approach (Huddleston 1970; Cattell 1973; Östman 1981; Quirk et al. 1985; McGregor 1995; Stenström 1997, 2005; Algeo 2006, pp. 293–303), quantitative studies of tag questions are undoubtedly few and far between although there are notable exceptions such as Nässlin (1984) on spoken British English, Biber et al. (1999) and Huddleston and Pullum (2002) on both spoken and written registers in British English, Tottie and Hoffmann (2006) on differences between British and American English, and Hoffmann et al. (2014) and Takahashi (2014) on inter-varietal variation of tag questions across Asian Englishes. Most of these studies focus on native English varieties such as British and American English and their uses of tag questions, and very little attention has been given to their different uses in other varieties of English, for example, spoken Brunei English (Cane 1996), Hong Kong English (HKE) (Todd and Hancock 1986; Cheng and Warren 2001; Hoffmann et al. 2014; Takahashi 2014) and Pakistani English (Hussain and Mahmood 2014). It is worth noting that all this research into non-native English varieties, used mostly in Southeast Asia, tends to suggest that it is very likely for non-native speakers of English to use the *isn't it* tag as a kind of universal or invariant or all-purpose tag question rather than employing it 'canonically' in Holmes' (1983) terminology—that is, modelling the revered polarity, verb and pronoun types from the main clause to which the tag question appended.

A tag question takes the form of an *anchor* and a (question) *tag* (after Huddleston and Pullum 2002, p. 891). Tottie and Hoffmann (2006, p. 308) state that the syntactic constituent to which a tag is attached has been referred to by a variety of terms in the literature such as *host clause*, *main clause*, *basic clause*, *matrix clause*, *stem clause* and *reference clause*, and they adopted the term 'anchor' in their paper without providing an explicit reason for so doing. It seems reasonable to say that the term 'anchor' is the best option in that more often than not, tags do not have to be attached to a clause; they 'are often added to a phrase or an incomplete clause' as in the utterance *Nice kitchen isn't it?* (Biber et al. 1999, p. 209).

In my view, it would be wise to use the term anchor so as to avoid any undesirable misconception that would could occur by employing other terminology such as, main clause.

A tag, on the other hand, is made up of an operator and a personal pronoun. According to Algeo (2006, pp. 293–294), there are two typical forms for a tag—either a *canonical* form with reverse polarity or an *anomalous* form with constant polarity. A positive (or affirmative) anchor operator essentially means that the tag operator is negative, and vice versa: *Julia can help, can't she?* (positive–negative) vs. *James can't help that, can he?* (negative–positive); in both examples, the subject of the anchor is co-referent with the personal pronouns *she* and *he*. These are examples for canonical forms where the polarity of the anchor is opposite to that of the tag but in anomalous forms the anchor can sometimes be identical to the tags in polarity. Algeo (2006, pp. 293–294) notes that while constant positive polarity is 'acceptable and not infrequent', it is 'rarer and disputed' to have consonant negative polarity: *You think that, do you?* (positive–positive) vs. *You oughtn't to say that now, oughtn't you?* (negative–negative).

The present chapter reports on a quantitative and qualitative study of the use of canonical and anomalous tag questions in HKE. I first provide an overview of major methodological issues that have arisen from the extraction of potential tag questions from the ICE-HK corpus (see section Chap. 1, Sect. 1.4 for the description of the corpus). I then discuss my corpus findings on the overall use of tag questions and their formal properties (polarity, verbs and pronouns in tags). The semantic and pragmatic functions of the tag questions will also be considered and analysed. The final section provides a summary of my findings and explores possible implications of the tendencies of tag questions in HKE.

2.2   Data Collection: Retrieving Tag Questions

The extraction of tag questions is not a trivial task for two reasons. First, tag questions coincide with other forms of interrogative clauses, for example, *It is good, isn't it?/Isn't it good?* Second, not all question tags occur in utterance-final position as in (1) and (2).

(1) And right on the almost on the final whistle just before United scored in injury time, I think mid-fielder Martin Cool got in a very good volley *didn't he* from some distance, but it really was whistling toward goal? (BNC-S)

(2) You wouldn't think, *would you*, that one tree could afford to lose. (ICE-HK:W2F-012#20:1)

One way of retrieving tag questions is, as recommended by Tottie and Hoffmann (2006, p. 285), to perform a 'purely lexical search (based on all of the possible auxiliary constructions in tags) for all possible question tag variants', an approach that involves 'a set of constraints to discard clearly irrelevant instances'. The first constraint is to exclude *wh*-questions, that is, 'instances with a *wh*-word (or a *wh*-word followed by a noun) immediately preceding the potential question tag' (Tottie and Hoffmann 2006, p. 285), as in (3)–(5):

(3) Hello, *how are* you? (BNC-S)

(4) *What number* is it? (BNC-S)

(5) *How many members* are there in in the organisation? (ICE-HK:S1A-008#23:1:A)

The second constraint is to disallow 'sentences with a verb immediately following the pronoun' (Tottie and Hoffmann 2006, p. 285), as in (6)–(8):

(6) Doesn't he *like* the vet? (BNC-S)

(7) Hasn't he *improved*? (BNC-S)

(8) Uh can you *speak* louder? (ICE-HK:S1B-011#109:1:D)

The third constraint is to disregard 'examples containing an adjective immediately following the pronoun of the potential question tag' (Tottie and Hoffmann 2006, p. 285), as in (9)–(11):

(9) Are they *comfortable*? (BNC-S)

(10) Are you *happy* to do it . . .? (BNC-S)

(11) Uh so what are you *busy* for? (ICE-HK:S1A-018#4:1:A)

In this current study, the same extraction procedures adopted in Tottie and Hoffmann (2006) have been used. The extraction procedures of the purely lexical search resulted in the retrieval of a total of 6,338 potential tag questions from ICE-HK. Manual inspection was then carried out so as to rule out false hits, resulting in a total of 197 relevant instances. My analysis therefore focusses on nearly 200 instances, some of which are tag questions with ellipsed anchors with deletion of TO BE, as shown in (12) to (14), which were treated as equivalents of regular tag questions. Given that subsets of the ICE-HK corpus, which are of varying sizes, were used for close inspection in my analysis, the corpus findings will be presented in terms of normalised frequency per 100,000 words. Throughout the book, the log-likelihood (LL) test has been used to determine the statistical significance of differences in frequency, making use of the UCREL Significance Test System available online at (http://corpora.lancs.ac.uk/sigtest/) developed by Andrew Hardie at Lancaster University.

(12) *Horrifying* isn't it? (ICE-HK:S1A-019#9:1:A)
(13) *Good point*, isn't it? (ICE-HK:S1A-069#X594:1:Z)
(14) *Weird*, isn't it? (ICE-HK:W1B-002#15:1)

2.3 Genre Variations in the Use of Tag Questions

An overview of the genre variations of tag questions in HKE is provided in Fig. 2.1 that shows the normalised frequency of occurrence of tag questions within twelve different text categories in the ICE-HK corpus (LL = 191.41, $p < 0.001$). As can be seen in Fig. 2.1, tag questions occur more than twice as frequently in spoken texts as in written texts. In the spoken data, over 50 % of tag questions can be found in spontaneous dialogue such as, telephone calls and broadcast interviews (i.e. *S1A* and *S1B*) and more than 10 % of tag questions occur in more formal monologue as in unscripted speeches and scripted talks (i.e. *S2A* and *S2B*). This corpus finding is congruent with the results of Biber et al. (1999), which looks into the distribution of question types (e.g. *wh-*question, *yes/no*-questions) across text types—according to Biber et al.

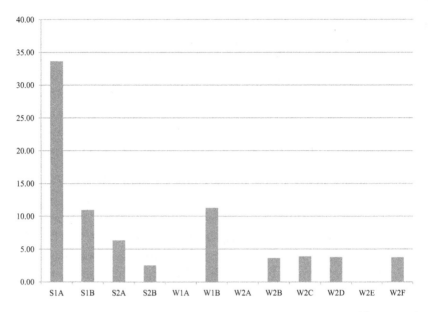

Fig. 2.1 Genre variation in tag questions in ICE-HK (in normalised frequency)

(1999, p. 211), 'about every fourth question in conversation is a question tag' because it is 'a frequent means of seeking agreement and keeping the conversation going'.

In the written texts, on the other hand, half of the tag questions occur in correspondence (*W1B*), which is comparatively more informal than other types of writing included in the ICE-HK corpus. It then does not come as a surprise that tag questions have zero occurrences in examination scripts (*W1A*), academic prose (*W2A*) and press editorials (*W2E*).

2.4   Patterns of Polarity in Tags

As briefly noted in Sect. 2.1, while a tag question can take a canonical form with reversed polarity, as in examples (15) to (18), it can also take an anomalous form with constant polarity, as in examples (19) to (21)

Positive–negative:

(15) Yeah *we are* the same kind of people *aren't we*? (ICE-HK:S1A-035#382:1:A)

(16) *He left, didn't he*? (ICE-HK:S1A-008#81:1:A)

Negative–positive:

(17) Yeah but *he doesn't* know it's technology *does he*? (ICE-HK:S1A-047#13:1:A)

(18) *He didn't* teach before *did he*? (ICE-HK:S1A-053#105:1:A)

Positive–positive:

(19) *It's* raining *is it*? (ICE-HK:S1A-023#X253:1:Z)

(20) *It's* a new building *is it*? (ICE-HK:S1A-021#50:1:B)

Negative–negative:

(21) Notice that *this is not* ordinary, not ordinary sentences *isn't it* (ICE-HK:S1B-019#238:1:A)

From the ICE-HK corpus, the most frequent choice of tag questions made by Hong Kong speakers of English has been found to be positive-negative polarity tag constructions (see Fig. 2.2; LL = 215.24, $p < 0.001$). However, this finding is not at all very surprising given the fact that native speakers of British and American English very commonly add tags to positive declarative clauses (Biber et al. 1999, p. 211; Tottie and Hoffmann, 2006, p. 289). In contrast, anomalous positive-positive constructions show a high frequency of occurrence in ICE-HK to the extent that they are almost as frequent as the canonical positive-negative polarity constructions (40 % vs. 56 %). This is somewhat surprising when compared to Tottie and Hoffmann's (2006, p. 290) observation that there is a rather low proportion (less than 10 %) of anomalous tag questions used in native Englishes. A closer look into this type of polarity in the corpus data is therefore necessary in order to explain the observed differences in the use of positive-positive tag questions between British

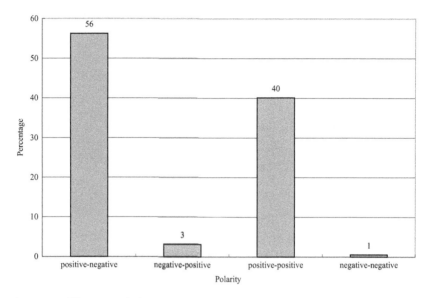

Fig. 2.2 Different polarity patterns in tag questions in ICE-HK

and American speakers and HKE speakers. It has been found that compared to British and American English, almost all of the 'non-standard' uses of tag questions in ICE-HK are of positive-positive polarity. There is only one exception where the tag construction with positive-positive polarity in HKE is used in a similar way as in native varieties of English by seeking 'confirmation of a statement whose truth is assumed' (Algeo 2006, p. 293), as shown in (22).

(22) Z: Did you do your so you you don't only did your you did your
    A-levels in Canada as well?
    B: No just the uhm HKCEE level
    Z: Uh *that's* O Level *is it?*
    A: Yup
    B: Yeah O Level yeah O Level
    (ICE-HK:S1A-010#204–208)

In example (22), speaker Z draws a conclusion from something speaker B has just said by producing a tag question that has the communicative purpose of confirming that conclusion that Z assumes to be true. As clearly shown in the following turns of the conversation above, it is indeed confirmed by both speakers A and B. This is the only instance found in the entire ICE-HK corpus that the positive-positive polarity is considered to be valid and in other cases in the corpus such a structure emerges as a non-standard and potentially new varietal feature for which the positive-negative polarity, which is more commonly used in standard varieties, would have been expected, as in examples (19) and (20), *It's raining isn't it?* and *It's a new building isn't it?*, respectively where the standard forms are used.

There is one instance of negative-negative tag construction (given in example (21) above), which has been proved to be common across Asian Englishes (Takahashi 2014). In native varieties of English, however, it is considered rare. For example, Quirk et al. (1985, p. 813) point out that such construction 'has not been clearly attested in actual use' and over two decades later Algeo (2006, p. 294) states that it is 'at best marginal . . . and exceptional in various ways'.

2.5   Variability in the Use of Operators and Pronouns

The various operators (i.e. auxiliaries and modal verbs) in question tags have also been examined in the present study. As illustrated in Fig. 2.3 (LL = 418.80, $p < 0.001$), the verb *TO BE* is the most frequent operator used in question tags in ICE-HK, followed by the verb *TO DO*. Some other operators are also commonly used in question tags, including the modal verbs *WILL, HAVE, CAN* and *SHALL*. While HKE resembles British and American English (Tottie and Hoffmann 2006, p. 291) in its use of operators in tag questions, there are still considerable discrepancies between HKE and the two native varieties of English when it comes to the combination of auxiliary, pronoun and optional *n't* in tag constructions.

As can be seen from Table 2.1, there are , in total, 30 different combinations of operators and personal pronouns in question tags found in the ICE-HK corpus, although most of them occur in very low

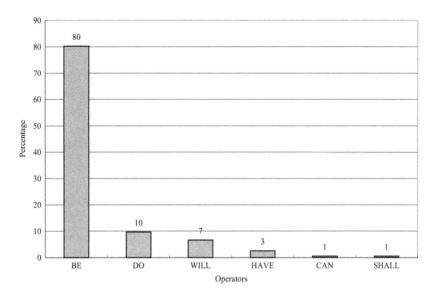

Fig. 2.3 Operators used in question tags in ICE-HK (in normalised frequency)

Table 2.1 Variation in the use of operators and pronouns in tag questions in ICE-HK

Tag	%	Rank	Tag	%	Rank
is it?	38.4	1	*couldn't it?*	0.5	8
isn't it?	31.6	2	*did he?*	0.5	8
aren't they?	3.7	3	*does he?*	0.5	8
isn't he?	2.6	4	*don't you?*	0.5	8
aren't you?	2.1	5	*hasn't it?*	0.5	8
wasn't it?	2.1	5	*haven't they?*	0.5	8
wouldn't it?	2.1	5	*is there?*	0.5	8
don't they?	1.6	6	*isn't there?*	0.5	8
have you?	1.6	6	*should we?*	0.5	8
didn't he?	1.1	7	*was it?*	0.5	8
didn't you?	1.1	7	*will they?*	0.5	8
do you?	1.1	7	*won't you?*	0.5	8
was I?	1.1	7	*would you?*	0.5	8
weren't you?	1.1	7	*wouldn't they?*	0.5	8
will you?	1.1	7	*wouldn't you?*	0.5	8

frequencies. With about 40 % of all occurrences of tag question in the corpus, *Is it?* is regarded as the top-ranking tag in HKE. This is in contrast with Tottie and Hoffmann's (2006) finding that *isn't it?* is the most common type in both British and American English. This stark contrast also seems to contradict the observation made by Todd and Hancock (1986) that the construction *isn't it?* should be considered as an all-purpose question tag that could be used after all kinds of anchor. However, from what can be gleaned from ICE-HK, *is it?* is the preferred choice of a universal question tag used in HKE where no attempt is made to produce a tag that would conform to the verb and subject used in the preceding anchor, as shown in (23) and (24). In fact, the universal question tag *is it?* is highly frequent in HKE, making up over 97 % of its total occurrences, as opposed to the remaining 3 per cent of *is it?* tags that are used canonically as in (25). While it has already been suggested that both *isn't it?* and *is it?* could be universal tags that are commonly used in conversational HKE (Cheng and Warren 2001, pp. 1427–1428), it is still unclear which one of these two question tags is the dominant type in HKE without solid quantitative evidence based on a corpus. As illustrated in (26), taken from ICE-HK, the tag *isn't* is also used universally, albeit not very frequently (about 13 times out of 60, or about 20 per cent of its total occurrences). In terms of frequency of occurrence, it would be reasonable to assume that *isn't it?* is a far less successful candidate as a universal tag than *is it?* at least in the ICE-HK corpus (20 % vs. 97 %).

(23) We have an interesting situation here, *is it?* (ICE-HK:W2F-019#205:1)
(24) And the people there is very poor *is it?* (ICE-HK:S1A-056#32:1:A)
(25) It isn't a good job, *is it?* (ICE-HK:S1A-036#X173:1:Z)
(26) You are now in Form Two, *isn't it?* (ICE-HK:S1A-085#X13:1:Z)

It is also important to point out that it is indeed very widespread in HKE that the operator and/or subject in tags do not match those used in anchors; it has been found that more than 80 % of tags in ICE-HK do not model on the anchor. This is an interesting finding that could potentially point to a unique feature of tag questions produced by Hong Kong speakers of English in that there is quite a high incidence of such uses of tag questions that clearly shows a totally unexpected combination of operators and subjects in the tags, as shown in examples (27) to (32).

(27) *Chinese people call* it bad luck well *aren't they?* (ICE-HK:S1A-030#X877:1:Z)

(28) *Can they* overlap anyway *don't they?* (ICE-HK:S1A-076#X395:1:Z)

(29) *You've* got twenty-five percent chance, *don't you?* (ICE-HK:S1A-036#X307:1:Z)

(30) *Bought* himself family car *isn't it?* (ICE-HK:S1A-014#X396:1:Z)

(31) But *there's* a new one coming up *isn't it?* (ICE-HK:S1A-022#X39:1:Z)

(32) *It's* somebody else's book or story *aren't they?* (ICE-HK:S1A-080#X543:1:Z)

There are, however, a few instances in the corpus that due to changes made by speakers during the course of the conversation, the operator in the question tag may be different from that in the preceding anchor. This is not unusual in native Englishes in that the change of subject or auxiliary could be well-justified in some context (Biber et al. 1999, p. 209); for instance, as shown in (33), the auxiliary is changed from the neutral future-referring *'ll* in the anchor to the hypothetical *would* in the tag. Note also that the tags in examples (34) and (35) are modelled on the operator and/or subject in the subordinate clause rather than on the operator and/or subject in the main clause. Huddleston and Pullum (2002, pp. 893–894) suggest that this is commonplace in native English where verbs of opinion such as *think, know* and *seem* are used in the main clause. In some cases where the mismatch occurs the speech-act function of the anchor tends to be shifted from seeking confirmation to making a request as shown in (36).

(33) Yeah but then *you'll* be bored *wouldn't you?* (ICE-HK:S1A-030#X255:1:Z)

(34) I know on the platforms of the train stations *they have* them *don't they?* (ICE-HK:S1A-030#X201:1:Z)

(35) I think *it's* just called CK *isn't it?* (ICE-HK:S1A-030#X425:1:Z)

(36) I feel it is great because when I go to Australia, *you can* drive me out everywhere, *won't you?* (ICE-HK:W1B-002#57:2)

2.6   The Classification of the Communicative Functions of Tags

The classification of the communicative functions of tags has been studied using various different approaches in previous studies. In the hope of providing a review of these approaches, in order to decide on the approach suitable for the current study, Table 2.2 offers a glimpse into the different empirically based classification systems that are derived from prior research into the functions of tags that substantially draws on authentic evidence (e.g. Holmes 1995; Biber et al. 1999; Tottie and Hoffmann 2006), while putting aside those approaches based on invented examples (e.g. Cattell 1973; Aijmer 1979) and those containing non-prototypical types of tag (e.g. McGregor 1995; Stenström 2005). In Table 2.2 different partitions are used so as to demonstrate partial overlap of the categories employed in these previous studies. Given that Algeo's (2006) system draws much of its inspirations from Tottie and Hoffmann (2006) it is not reviewed here.

By seeking information from the addressee, Holmes' (1995) *epistemic modal* tags correspond with *informational* tags in Tottie and Hoffmann's (2006) and Biber et al.'s (1999) systems and the tag was therefore included in the analytical framework adopted in this study. Holmes' (1995) uses the term *facilitative* to refer to tags that are used to elicit confirmation and engage the addressee interactively in conversation; similarly, tags of this type are also found in Biber et al.'s (1999) and Tottie and Hoffmann's (2006) systems. However, there is a differential

Table 2.2 Previous classification systems of functions of tags

Holmes (1995)	Biber et al. (1999)	Tottie and Hoffmann (2006)
Epistemic modal	Elicit information	Informational
	Elicit agreement or confirmation	Confirmatory
Facilitative		Facilitating
Softening		
	Express a comment	Attitudinal
Challenging		Peremptory
		Aggressive

treatment in prior studies concerning *confirmatory* tags ('the speaker is not sure of what s/he says, wants confirmation') and *facilitating* tags ('the speaker is sure of the truth of what s/he says but wants to involve listener') in that while Tottie and Hoffmann (2006, pp. 300–301) make a clear distinction between the two, Biber et al. (1999) conflate the two categories into one that is primarily used to appeal to the addressee for confirmation. Since a closer look at the function of these two categories reveals that they function in more or less the same way, Biber et al.'s (1999) approach was adopted while retaining the label *confirmatory* taken from Tottie and Hoffmann (2006) as a cover term for both facilitating and confirmatory uses. On the other hand, there is one functional category that is non-existent in these two systems and only appears in Holmes' (1995) scheme, that is, the *softening* category. As this category is only set up in Holmes' study specifically to examine politeness in women's talk, it was considered to be irrelevant and therefore excluded from the analytical framework of the present study. Since both Biber et al. (1999, p. 209) and Tottie and Hoffmann (2006) have acknowledged the function of tags to express a comment, the *attitudinal* label (originally proposed by Tottie and Hoffmann 2006) was considered to be promising and therefore also included in this study. Additionally, it is interesting to note that two other categories are also devised by Tottie and Hoffmann's (2006): *peremptory* and *aggressive*. These largely correspond to Holmes' *challenging* tags while the peremptory tag question typically follows a statement of obvious truth and is most likely intended to close off further discussion of topic, the aggressive tag follows a statement whose truth the addressee cannot know and thus functions as provocation. Although Algeo (2006, p. 298) considers these two tags to be 'specifically British', they were also included for analysis in the HKE data, possibly revealing the influence of the historical input variety on HKE despite the expectation that the chances of their occurrence would be rather slim.

As a result, a total of five categories (*informational, confirmatory, attitudinal, peremptory* and *aggressive*) were taken from previous research and included in the classification system used in the present study. Under this analytical framework, different functions of tags were examined with reference to their linguistic contexts. It is worth mentioning that while intonation (part of the verbal context) could potentially be a vital area for

2 Tag Questions   45

investigating the functions of tag questions (Coates 1996, p. 196; Huddleston and Pullum 2002, pp. 894–895), the effect of intonation on the interpretation of tags and their functions has not been analysed due to the fact that only a very small number of sample sound files are available for download from the ICE website and they have yet to be prosodically annotated to include information on intonation. Hence in this study the analysis of the functions of tags was entirely based on linguistic contexts. Examples from the ICE-HK corpus on the classification of the functions of tags are shown in (37) to (42).

Informational (ask for information):

(37) B: I just don't have enough money to go to both trip [sic].
    A: Yeah.
    Z: Can they overlap anyway *don't they*?
    B: No. They don't.
    (ICE-HK:S1A-076#393–397)
(38) A: You always go in there.
    Z: Yeah.
    Z: Uhm uhm.
    A: You have kids *isn't*?
    A: You have kids have you?
    Z: What?
    A: You have kids is it? Kids, chil- children.
    Z: Yeah, I have two.
    (ICE-HK:S1A-050#279–287)

Confirmatory (seek confirmation and expect involvement from the addressee):

(39) Z: Uh bad influence ((both laugh))
    A: Yeah we are the same kind of people *aren't we*?
    Z: Yeah but money is not everything you know.
    (ICE-HK:S1A-035#X381–383)
(40) A: We were supposed to be here.
    A: Yeah they got really nice office *haven't they*?
    B: Yeah it's a- actually it's really nice.

(ICE-HK:S1A-100#349–351)

Attitudinal (express a comment or emphasise what the speaker says):

(41) A: Because I you know I- I enjoy being in the Catholic Society
much more.
Z: Okay.
Z: Oh yes you are Catholic *aren't you*?
A: Yes.
(ICE-HK:S1A-018#216–219)
(42) A: He didn't teach before *did he*?
A: He was in charge of-
Z: In charge of the- I think he still is
(ICE-HK:S1A-053#105–108)

Peremptory (follow statement of obvious truth and close off further
discussion):

No instances were found.

Aggressive (act as insult or provocation):

No instances were found.

As illustrated in Fig. 2.4 (LL = 313.17, $p < 0.001$), over 90 % of the
total tags in ICE-HK are *confirmatory* and *attitudinal* tags. The informational category is used very infrequently and constitutes only 5 % of the
total tags. In terms of the distribution of the different functional categories, HKE bears a striking resemblance to British and American English:
while Coates (1996, p. 306) notes 16 % of tag questions for seeking
information and the remaining 84 % for other functions, Tottie and
Hoffmann (2006, p. 301) report that more than 90 % of their tag
questions elicit confirmation and emphasise speaker's opinion in conversation and just 3 % are information seeking. As expected, the peremptory

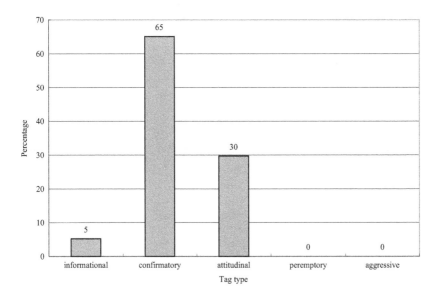

Fig. 2.4 Distribution of different functional categories of tags in ICE-HK

and aggressive tags, which are specifically British, are non-existent in the ICE-HK data.

In prior research, it has been suggested that there might be a correlation between the interpretation of tags and their polarity types: for example, Huddleston and Pullum (2002) characterise constant-polarity tags as carrying 'an emotive meaning of disapproval, reproach, belligerence, ... sarcasm' (2002, p. 895). Similarly, Quirk et al. (1985, p. 812) note that constant-polarity tags are 'sarcastically contradictory'. Specifically, British English might perhaps provide some evidence for this correlation in the use of the constant polarity tag construction (see Kimps 2005, cited in Tottie and Hoffmann 2006, p. 302). In HKE, however, it is not entirely clear whether it can be considered as one of the new varietal characteristics of tag questions. As noted earlier in Sect. 2.4, over 99 % of constant-polarity tags have been found in ICE-HK for which reversed polarity is the preferred option in native varieties such as British and American English. It would therefore be reasonable to suggest that the correlation between polarity types and pragmatic functions of tag questions seems to be rather tenuous in the context of HKE.

2.7   Substrate Influence from Cantonese

In Cantonese, there are three kinds of tag question characterised by the use of three different question tags (Matthews and Yip 2011, pp. 366–367). The first kind of tag question in Cantonese with the question tag *hai6-m4hai6* are typically used to confirm the truth of a proposition in much the same way as the confirmatory tags function in the English language, as in example (43). However, the Cantonese tag is 'invariant in form, translating *aren't you?*, *don't they?*, etc.' (Matthews and Yip 2011, p. 367).

(43)	nei5	zou6	ji1sang1	hai6	m4hai6	aa
	you	work	doctor	right		SFP[1]
	'You're a doctor, aren't you?'					

For the record, the other two kinds of tag question in Cantonese do not have any direct equivalents in the English language; *hou2-m4hou2* is attached as a tag to requests or suggestions, meaning 'okay?' whereas *dak1-m4dak1* is used as a tag to elicit consent or approval.

(44)	ngo5dei6	zou2di1	zau2	hou2-m4hou2	a?
	we	early-ish	leave	okay	SFP
	'Let's leave early, shall we?'				

(45)	ngo5	ting1jat6	wan2	nei5	king1haa5	dak1-m4dak1	aa?
	I	tomorrow	seek	you	chat.a.while	okay-not.okay	SFP
	'I'll come and talk to you tomorrow, okay?'						

The dominant use of confirmatory tags in HKE can indeed be explained by the substrate influence from Cantonese in which the same kind of tag question can be found (cf. Parviainen 2016). Similarly, given that the Cantonese tag *hai6-m4hai6* is used invariantly for confirmatory purposes, it does not come as a surprise that both *is it?* and *isn't it?* are used as universal tags and occur remarkably more frequently than all of the other forms in HKE as clearly shown in the ICE-HK corpus data above.

---

[1] The abbreviation *SFP* stands for sentence-final particle.

2.8   Conclusion

In this chapter, tag questions have been closely examined in HKE. From the ICE-HK corpus data, it is evident that spoken text, particularly face-to-face and telephone conversations, unscripted speeches and scripted talks, show a high incidence of tag questions, whereas in formal writing for example, academic prose, examination scripts and press editorials, tag questions are very rarely used. The verb TO BE has been found to be the most common operator in question tags in ICE-HK; the verbs TO DO and WILL (modal verb) come second and third, followed by other verbs such as TO HAVE, CAN (modal verb) and SHALL (modal verb). These tendencies about the tag questions in HKE tally perfectly with those in native varieties of English such as British and American English. However, there are also significant differences in the use of tag questions between HKE and these two native varieties ofEnglish. While HKE demonstrates a clear preference for the tag construction *Is it?*, the *isn't it?* construction is predominant among British and American speakers. Although there are minor departures from the main pattern of tag formation in all these varieties, more than 80 % of tags in ICE-HK are new varietal uses, showing a mismatch between the tag and the anchor in terms of verb and subject. In the analysis of the semantic and pragmatic functions of tag questions, the functions of eliciting confirmation and participation from other speakers as well as emphasising what the speaker says are the most common, while the function of genuine requests for information is used far less frequently.

In terms of overall frequency of occurrence, tag questions are less represented in HKE(Cheng and Warren 2001, pp. 1434–1436). In the whole ICE-HK Corpus, which contains 1 million words, there are only about 200 genuine examples of tag question. Admittedly, this very low overall frequency might be explained by the relatively small size of the ICE-HK corpus used in this study (as compared to the 100-million-word British National Corpus, for example). Another potential reason is related to the rather limited functions of tag questions used by Hong Kong speakers of English: there is a possibility that 'tags are certainly not the only means available to speakers to do such things' as obtaining information, seeking confirmation or emphasising what they are saying (Cheng and Warren 2001, p. 1437), although further research is needed to explore what precisely those 'means' are in conversational English. As shown in the present study, there is a distinction between regular tag questions such as *aren't they?*, *do you?*, and invariant/invariable tag questions that refer to 'a range of other expressions which can be tagged on to a clause, with much the same effect as a question tag' (Biber et al. 1999, p. 210), including *yeah? eh? okay? right? innit? don't you think? hm?* (Biber et al. 1999, p. 210; Stenström 2005). Algeo (2006, pp. 302–303) notes that these invariant tags 'are occasionally used in English' and 'nonstandard'. While the full extent of the invariant tags has not been the focus of the present study, which is primarily a comparison of relatively 'standard' features of native and non-native English varieties, a preliminary analysis of one of the invariant tags, *right?*, in ICE-HK reveals that this is favoured by Hong Kong speakers over a regular tag question as in examples (46) to (49). The invariant tag forms could serve as an interesting avenue for further research by considering systematic differences in the use of these forms between HKE and standard varieties of English such as British and American English.

(43) You've already finished your first year Uni's life, *right?* (ICE-HK: W1B-002#65:2)

(44) Today is your birthday, *right?* (ICE-HK:W1B-002#196:8)

(45) I think you can get a pass in it, *right?* (ICE-HK:W1B-004#106:1)

(46) We can't waste any of our valuable time, *right?* (ICE-HK:W1B-014#205:15)

Despite the fact that the occurrence of non-native tag question production as a new varietal feature reported in ICE-HK is very high, reaching up to over 80 %, Hong Kong speakers of English would probably find it hard to use a tag construction in conversation especially under real-time constraints in the course of speaking, as evidenced by a rather low overall frequency of tag questions as noted above. This has also led to the use of *is it?* as a universal tag and *right?* as an alternative, possibly influenced by the substrate language Cantonese. In particular, the new uses tend to emerge from the form rather than the function of tag questions: it has been found that the commonly used semantic and pragmatic functions of tag questions (i.e. seeking confirmation, emphasising what is said and asking for information) in HKE coincide with those in native Englishes. The major difference in the formal properties of tag questions appears to be that question tags used in HKE do not model on the anchor with respect to verb and pronoun as in the native English varieties. Unlike British and American English, there is a predilection for using combinations of verbs and pronouns in question tags that are different from those in the anchor in HKE.

References

Aijmer, Karin. 1979. The Function of Tag Questions in English. In *Papers from the Fifth Scandinavian Conference of Linguistics*, ed. Tore Pettersson, 9–17. Lund, Sweden: Acta Universitatis Lundensis and Stockholm: Almqvist and Wiksell.

Algeo, John. 2006. *British or American English? A Handbook of Word and Grammar Patterns*. Cambridge: Cambridge University Press.

Biber, Douglas, Stig Johansson, Geoffrey Leech, Susan Conrad, and Edward Finegan. 1999. *Longman Grammar of Spoken and Written English*. Harlow, UK: Longman.

Cane, Graeme. 1996. Syntactic Simplification and Creativity in Spoken Brunei English. In *Language Use and Language Change in Brunei Darussalam*, ed. Peter Martin, Conrad Ozog, and Gloria Poedjosoedarmo, 209–222. Athens, Ohio: Ohio University Center for International Studies.

Cattell, Ray. 1973. Negative Transportation and Tag Questions. *Language* 49 (3): 612–639.

Cheng, Winnie, and Martin Warren. 2001. 'She Knows About Hong Kong Than You Do Isn't It?': Tags in Hong Kong Conversational English. *Journal of Pragmatics* 33(9): 1419–1439.

Coates, Jennifer. 1996. *Women Talk*. Cambridge, MA: Blackwell.

Hoffmann, Sebastian, Anne-Katrin Blass, and Joybrato Mukherjee. 2014. Canonical Tag Questions in Asian Englishes: Forms, Functions, and Frequencies in Hong Kong English, Indian English, and Singapore English. In *The Oxford Handbook of World Englishes*, ed. Markku Filppula, Juhani Klemola, and Devyani Sharma. Oxford: Oxford University Press.

Holmes, Janet. 1983. The Functions of Tag Questions. *English Language Research Journal* 3(1983): 40–65.

———. 1995. *Women, Men and Politeness*. White Plains, NY: Longman.

Huddleston, Rodney. 1970. Two Approaches to the Analysis of Tags. *Journal of Linguistics* 6(1970): 215–222.

Huddleston, Rodney, and Geoffrey Pullum. 2002. *The Cambridge Grammar of the English Language*. Cambridge: Cambridge University Press.

Hussain, Zahida, and Muhammad Asim Mahmood. 2014. Invariant Tag Questions in Pakistani English: A Comparsion with Native and Other Non-Native Englishes. *Asian Englishes* 16(3): 229–238.

Matthews, Stephen, and Virginia Yip. 2011. *Cantonese: A Comprehensive Grammar*. 2nd ed. London and New York: Routledge.

McGregor, William. 1995. The English 'Tag Question': A New Analysis, Is(n't) It? In *On Subject and Theme: A Discourse Functional Perspective*, ed. Ruqaiya Hasan and Peter Fries, 91–121. Amsterdam: John Benjamins.

Nässlin, Siv. 1984. *The English Tag Question: A Study of Sentences Containing Tags of the Type Isn't It?, Is It?* (Stockholm Studies in English, 60). Stockholm: Almqvist and Wiksell.

Östman, Jan Ola. 1981. A Functional Approach to English Tags. *Studia Anglica Posnaniensia* 13(1981): 3–16.

Parviainen, Hanna. 2016. The Invariant Tag *Isn't It* in Asian Englishes. *World Englishes* 35(1): 98–117.

Quirk, Randolph, Sidney Greenbaum, Geoffrey Leech, and Jan Svartvik. 1985. *A Comprehensive Grammar of the English Language*. London: Longman.

Stenström, Anna-Brita. 1997. Tags in Teenage Talk. In *From Ælfric to the New York Times: Studies in English Corpus Linguistics*, ed. Udo Fries, Viviane Müller, and Peter Schneider, 139–147. Amsterdam: Rodopi.

———. 2005. Teenagers' Tags in London and Madrid. In *Contexts—Historical, Social, Linguistic* (Studies in Celebration of Toril Swan), ed. Kevin McCafferty, Tove Bull, and Kristin Killie, 279–291. Bern, Switzerland: Peter Lang.

Takahashi, Mariko. 2014. A Comparative Study of Tag Questions in Four Asian Englishes from a Corpus-Linguistic Approach. *Asian Englishes* 16(2): 101–124.

Todd, Loreto, and Ian Hancock. 1986. *International English Usage*. London: Groom Helm.

Tottie, Gunnel, and Sebastian Hoffmann. 2006. Tag Questions in British and American English. *Journal of English Linguistics* 34(4): 283–311.

3

Collective Nouns

Abstract In the ICE-HK corpus, Wong examines collective nouns used in Hong Kong English, with particular reference to subject-verb agreement/concord patterns. The chapter discusses singular collective nouns as subjects and how the following verb or pronoun agrees with them in number as well as assessing previous claims that concord variations with collective nouns are semantically or pragmatically motivated by the traditional 'collectivity vs individuality' principle and the semantics of the following verb phrase. Wong reveals that singular concord is the preferred choice in the majority of the corpus data, and that convention rather than semantic/pragmatic motivation plays a crucial role in concord patterns with collective nouns, with individual collective nouns showing their own preferences for a singular or plural form.

Keywords Collective nouns • Subject-verb agreement • Concord • Semantic/pragmatic motivation • Hong Kong English

3.1   Introduction

The most intriguing characteristics of collective nouns such as *committee, staff, council* is concord pattern: there are two types of concord pattern, that is, singular and plural concord, in which the collective noun has to agree with a verb where the noun is the subject, or to agree with a later pronoun. Across different varieties of English, there is a clear variation in the use of concord pattern (Bauer 2002, p. 50) in that while plural concord is preferred by British English speakers, singular concord is the only option among American English speakers (Biber et al. 1999, p. 19). While concord pattern of collective nouns serves to mark the difference between British and American English, the variation in singular and plural concord with singular collective nouns has largely been neglected in Asian Englishes, except for Singaporean and Philippine English (Hundt 2006). This chapter therefore aims to fill this gap by exploring singular collective nouns as subjects and investigating factors that play a role in the agreement in number of these nouns with the following verb or pronoun based on the data taken from the ICE-HK corpus presenting both quantitative and qualitative findings.

3.2   Data Collection: Extraction of Collective Nouns

To achieve the research objectives, the procedures of extraction of collective nouns proposed by Hundt (2006, pp. 212–214) were adopted in this study for retrieving collective nouns. In keeping with the model used in Hundt (2006), most of the nouns listed in Quirk et al. (1985, p. 316) were included in the extraction and only those that occurred very infrequently in the 1-million-word ICE-HK corpus (e.g. *jury* and *enemy*) were disregarded. The procedure resulted in the retrieval of examples of totally thirty-five collective nouns for analysis:

> *army, association, audience, board, cast, clan, class, club, college, commission, committee, community, company, corporation, council, couple, crew, crowd,*

department, family, federation, gang, generation, government, group, institute, majority, ministry, minority, opposition, party, population, staff, team, university.

Moreover, only the singular form (e.g. *crew, audience*) of a collective noun was being considered and the plural form ignored (e.g. *crews, audiences*) (cf. Aremo, 2005). Additionally, only finite, present-tense lexical verbs in the indicative mood that explicitly mark a distinction in number were examined in the present study. Hence, the resultant retrieval obtained corpus examples of collective nouns in combination with finite verbs and personal pronouns that exhibit singular and plural concord patterns as shown in examples (1) and (2), while neglecting all corpus instances of collective nouns that are followed by non-finite verbs that co-occur with *to*-infinitive as in (3) or an auxiliary , for example, *will, may, must* as in examples (4) and (5) and those instances involving finite auxiliary or main verbs with past reference as in examples (6) and (7).

(1) I will stay if the *Army allows* me to stay, you know. (ICE-HK:S1A-052#X604:1:Z)
(2) Uh for the uh for the older *generation they* like to go to visit temples uhm everywhere. (ICE-HK:S1A-008#123:1:A)
(3) Billions of dollars in financial pledges was a start, but Afghanistan also needs stability and security, and it is up to the world *community to* ensure these are in place. (ICE-HK:W2E-001#111:6)
(4) Well the *majority* of local people *will* stay in Hong Kong just I am not quite sure what you feel about it because many of our visitors ah told us that why are many people or all all the people are leaving Hong Kong and moved to our ah home country ahem because I think many of the visitors uh have found more and more Chinese neighbours near them (ICE-HK:S2A-031#89:1:A)
(5) But I think the curriculum development *committee must* be looking into this uhm uh uhm in into this subject. (ICE-HK:S1B-049#154:2:B)
(6) The *majority* of cases, however, *had* not been diagnosed previously. (ICE-HK:W2A-024#108:1)

(7) The *committee decided* measures to control pornographic videotapes and laser discs should include heavier fines. (ICE-HK:W2C-013#109:4)

The retrieval procedure also excluded those corpus examples involving invariant tags (e.g. *is it/isn't it*). Following the suggestion made in Levin (2001, p. 51), sentences with unclear referents from the spoken texts of ICE-HK were also discarded. On the other hand, the data collected included sentences with relative clauses introduced by *which* and *who* followed by a singular or plural verb form, as shown in examples (8) and (9) as well as sentences with collective nouns appearing as part of a proper noun (e.g. *the British Council, the SAR government*) as in example (9).

(8) In addition, for over eighty-five percent of the secondary school *population, who learn* the science and humanities in English, a large of proportion of their work on these subjects is actually tackling language. (ICE-HK:S2B-028#9:1:A)

(9) The Industry and Technology Development *Council which was* established earlier this year will advise the government on what additional resources should be considered. (ICE-HK:S1B-057#68:1:B)

Where there were corpus examples involving mixed agreement (i.e. the co-occurrence of a collective noun with a singular verb and a plural pronoun), they were considered in this study as single instances of mixed concord, as exemplified in examples (10) and (11).

(10) So where*'s* the closest *crew* that I can call *them* back to the office, okay? (ICE-HK:S2A-057#74:1:A)

(11) When the *company is* ready to send the application form, then *they*'ll send it. (ICE-HK:S1A-012#X27:1:Z)

3.3   Motivations Underlying Concord Variability of Collective Nouns

To account for the way in which a collective noun is followed by a particular verb form, prior studies have focussed on semantic and/or pragmatic motivations. Concord with collective nouns is widely believed to be dictated by a principle that the use of a plural verb is typically triggered by the view of the individuals belonging to a group denoted by the collective noun whereas the use of a singular verb is generally associated with the view of considering the group as a coherent unit. Moreover, concord variation also appears to be determined by the semantics of the verb phrase. As noted above, regional variations across varieties of English, notably British and American English, have also been shown to involve the preferential use of a particular verb form with collective nouns. In this section, apart from providing an overview of the relevant previous literature on all these factors, concord variability of collective nouns will be explored with the help of the ICE-HK data.

3.3.1   Traditional Dichotomy Between Collectivity and Individuality

Arguably, the first comprehensive description of the dichotomy between the collectivity and individuality in connection with collective nouns was provided by Quirk et al. (1985, p. 316): 'the singular stresses the nonpersonal collectivity of the group, and the plural stresses the personal individuality within the group'. According to this principle, verbal/pronominal agreement with collective nouns is principally motivated by some underlying semantic/pragmatic factors in that the singular form is preferred when the individuals/items signalled by the collective noun are considered as a single whole, while the plural form is used when the individuals/items are construed separately as parts of the group. Indeed, this principle has been widely accepted ever since it was first conceived. It has been used in a majority of traditional grammars to account for concord variations among collective nouns; see, for example, *Collins Cobuild English Grammar* (1990, p. 16); Leech and Svartvik (1994,

p. 261); Greenbaum (1996, p. 104); Bache and Davidsen-Nielsen (1997, p. 395); Biber et al. (1999, p. 188); Dekeyser et al. (1999, p. 125); and Huddleston and Pullum (2002, p. 502). However popular this principle has been, the greatest difficulty in applying this principle is that it is almost 'impossible to interpret or judge the examples objectively' (Depraetere 2003, p. 106). Using naturally occurring data retrieved from the British English components of the then Bank of English corpus at Collins Cobuild, Depraetere (2003) contends that although semantic and/or pragmatic motivations undoubtedly determine concord patterns with collective nouns to a certain extent (as will be demonstrated below with corpus data from ICE-HK), their significance in the explanation was found to be less important than previously acknowledged in traditional grammars. Rather, he suggests that convention plays a far more pivotal role: in other words, particular collective nouns could show a predilection for either a singular or a plural verb that could not be explained by semantic and/or pragmatic factors alone; the preferences are highly likely to be governed by convention. In comparison with Depraetere's (2003) quantitative findings of collective nouns in British English, based on the ICE-HK corpus evidence, a similar patterning of concord has also been found in HKE's collective nouns.

As shown in Table 3.1, a majority of collective nouns (twenty seven out of thirty five or almost 80 %) demonstrate a clear preference for singular concord, while only a handful of collective nouns is used with plural concord. In some cases such as *army, board, club, corporation, crowd, federation, gang, institute* and *ministry*, the choice of singular concord is exclusively used, where the focus is explicitly on the group as a whole rather than on the individuals making up the group. Some examples are given as follows:

(12) Accordingly, the *board has* agreed to amend the first schedule to the Pharmacy and Poisons Regulations to achieve tighter control. (ICE-HK:S1B-059#88:1:G)
(13) A *crowd* of people *was* gathering at the centre of Pacific Place. (ICE-HK:W2F-004#115:2)

Table 3.1 Collective nouns and their concord patterns

	Singular concord (%)	Plural concord (%)	Mixed concord (%)
army	100	0	0
board	100	0	0
club	100	0	0
corporation	100	0	0
crowd	100	0	0
federation	100	0	0
gang	100	0	0
institute	100	0	0
ministry	100	0	0
community	95	5	0
department	95	5	0
university	95	5	0
government	94.8	5.2	0
council	91.9	8.1	0
committee	90.9	9.1	0
association	90.5	9.5	0
party	86.5	13.5	0
class	86.4	13.6	0
company	86.2	12.3	1.5
family	86	14	0
college	83.3	16.7	0
cast	75	25	0
crew	75	0	25
team	72.7	27.3	0
commission	66.7	33.3	0
population	66.7	33.3	0
group	65.5	34.5	0
staff	28	72	0
generation	23.5	70.6	5.9
couple	20	80	0
audience	14.3	85.7	0
majority	11.1	88.9	0
minority	0	100	0
clan	0	0	0
opposition	0	0	0

(14) Although the *Federation was* established in 1901, it was not until 9 July 1900 the Commonwealth of Australia constitution Act 1900 was enacted. (ICE-HK:W1A-010#61:1)

(15) The *gang has* also been sending its fake credit cards overseas. (ICE-HK:S2B-016#79:2:A)

(16) I think I think the PRC officials mainly the *Ministry* of Finance *is* extremely aware of that. (ICE-HK:S2A-023#106:5:A)

For some collective nouns such as *community, department, university, government, council, committee, association, party, class, company, family* and *college*, singular concord occurs over 80 % of the time. Of these collective nouns, a vast majority appear in proper nouns referring to decision-making official bodies and organisations, for example, the Immigration Department, University of Hong Kong, the Chinese government, the Hong Kong Productivity Council, the SAR Preparatory Committee, the Hong Kong Amateur Swimming Association, the Liberal Party and the New Asia College. These collective nouns, as Biber et al. (1999, p. 247) point out, behave in a similar way to proper nouns in general and thus do not allow for any contrast in number. Singular concord is an unmarked form when it comes to selecting a particular verb form following these nouns.

(17) The Social Welfare *Department has* no specific programme to help the husbands. (ICE-HK:W2B-014#90:1)

(18) The Hong Kong *government is* therefore not subjected to the same degree of spending pressures that confront the governments of many democratic countries. (ICE-HK:W2A-017#41:1)

(19) The Democratic *Party is* expected to lose further ground in the next Legco election. (ICE-HK:W2B-011#130:2)

(20) Wah Yan *College was* founded by Mr Peter Tsui in 1919 in Hollywood Road with no more than a handful pupils at its inception. (ICE-HK:W2B-010#82:1)

On the contrary, a small number of collective nouns such as *team, population* and *group* is associated with both singular and plural concord, although singular concord is still more commonly used. It is worth noting that those collective nouns with very low frequency (less than 5 %) such as *cast*, *crew* and *commission* are not taken into consideration, despite the fact that they pattern similarly with *team*, *population* and *group*.

(21) Dupont sales *team is* best described as an elite sales team which is characterised by members' high education level. (ICE-HK:S1B-004#28:1:B)

(22) With all their expensive gizmos, the Hong Kong Observatory *team* just *haven't* been making the right calls lately. (ICE-HK:W2B-022#2:1)

(23) Our working *population is* also projected to grow as well so that will uh take off part of the impact and also part of the uh proposals. (ICE-HK:S1B-044#18:1:A)

(24) Half the world's *population live* within five hours flying time of Hong Kong. (ICE-HK:S2B-050#26:1:A)

When combining with the prepositional phrase *of* + plural noun, the collective noun *group* differs from others in that it is considered as exemplifying the '*of*-collective' construction (Biber et al. 2002, p. 61). While the plural noun following *group* could potentially name a set of people, animals and objects, for example, the major collocation pattern that was attested in the ICE-HK corpus is one with 'people' as the plural noun as in the following examples.

(25) So so we're still talking a very large *group of people* who *rely* on the society to help them. (ICE-HK:S1B-048#141:2:A)

(26) Church is a place where a *group of believers gather* together to carry out the regular religious ceremonials. (ICE-HK:W1A-007#13:1)

(27) A *group of girls were* running behind the ball. (ICE-HK:W2F-004#42:1)

In the ICE-HK corpus, plural concord is predominantly used with six collective nouns: *staff, generation, couple, audience, majority* and *minority*. These collective nouns 'in themselves strongly suggest number' (Levin 2001, p. 147) and thus prefer plural concord over singular concord. More specifically, the collective noun *staff* is used with plural concord over 70 % of the time in HKE in much the same way as in British English (over

80 % of the time; see Biber et al. 1999, p. 188). On the other hand, *audience* varies remarkably in the two varieties of English. While plural concord is the preferred option to be used with the collective noun *audience* in HKE singular concord is frequently used in British English (Biber et al. 1999, p. 188).

(28) But I think it's partly because the older *generation want* the sense of being taking care of. (ICE-HK:S1A-028#449:1:B)

(29) The *majority* of these indicators *pertain* either to the proportion of the population having or not having a specific quality. (ICE-HK: W2A-015#37:1)

(30) Their consultancy *staff come* from a wide range of science and business backgrounds. (ICE-HK:S2B-042#118:3:A)

(31) Uhm well I think the *staff are* nice. (ICE-HK:S1A-079#X294:1:Z)

(32) Western *audience are* impressed by it because it wasn't one of those kungfu flicks that reduce the plot to a sideshow for the special effects. (ICE-HK:S2B-033#9:1:A)

(33) But even for for popular theatre like that they they will eventually feel may be under pressure may be because the *audience want* to see they want to to do something along the line as well. (ICE-HK:S1A-013#57:1:A)

Gleaned from the above corpus evidence, we could safely arrive at the conclusion that individual collective nouns do demonstrate preferences in their agreement with their following verbs. It now becomes clear that the commonly held traditional principle is too simplistic when it stipulates that a singular verb should be used with a collective noun when the focus is on collectivity and a plural verb should be used when the focus is on individuality. Rather, convention seems to be a more important factor in explaining the concord patterns of collective nouns. It is thus hardly surprising that another semantic motivation—namely, the semantics of the verb phrase—does not offer a promising explanation either, which is to be discussed in the next section.

3.3.2 The Semantic Classification of Lexical Verbs

The correlation between the semantic classification of lexical verbs and the concord patterns of collective nouns has been discussed by Huddleston (1988, p. 242), who points out that the plural form of a lexical verb (e.g. *disagree, leave, quarrel*) that inherently implies differentiation is highly likely to be used after a collective noun. Conversely, if a lexical verb presupposes decomposition/categorisation of unity (e.g. *consist of, be gathered, be dispersed*) then it is most likely to be used in the singular form. In line with the collectivism vs individualism principle as noted above, any verb that highlights individuals or 'personal things like deciding, hoping or wanting' (Swan, 1995, p. 526) is preferably used in the plural. While these intuitive observations appear to provide plausible explanations for concord patterning of collective nouns, they are flawed in view of attested language use in a sufficiently large representative corpus. For example, drawing on corpus evidence from the then Bank of English corpus (British English sections only; totalling roughly 40 million words), Depraetere (2003) insightfully points out that concord variations of collective nouns could not be sufficiently governed by the semantics of the verb phrase. In his corpus-based study of examining eight more fine-grained semantic subcategories of the verb phrase than those in previous literature, Depraetere (2003, pp. 116–123) sets out to pin down the verb form (singular or plural) for a particular verb choice: (1) a singular form tends to be used when the verb refers to physical attributes or states associated with a group of individuals (example 34a); (2) where the verb refers to an involuntary process that the group undergoes, a singular form is preferred (example 34b); (3) a plural from is likely to be used if the verb denotes (physical) activities carried out individuals (example 34c); (4) where the verb denotes feelings experienced by individuals, a plural form is likely to be used (example 34d); (5) a singular verb is preferred in cases where a mental activity expressed by the verb applies to the whole group (example 34e); (6) verbs that express the sense of unity (*divide, be composed of,* etc.) are likely to appear in the singular form (example 34f); (7) a plural form is favoured where the verbs indicate diversity (example 34g); and (8) a plural verb is the preferred choice where there is a mention of body parts as these physical attributes are characteristic of animate beings as opposed to institutions (example 34h).

(34) a. singular verb form for physical attributes/states of groups:
Well I think that probably is because the current *population has* all been <u>born</u> under the you know rule of the British from the very earliest memories that you would have all you can think about is what it is like to live in a uh territory that is uhm under the rule of of you know foreign country half way around the world. (ICE-HK: S1A-073#X40:1:Z)

b. singular verb form for involuntary processes undergone by groups:
So because there is not enough land *population <u>grows</u>* so fast so we need to build more houses in the green belt in the wild area. (ICE-HK:S1B-017#137:1:A)

c. plural verb form for physical activities performed by individuals:
Because most of our Hong Kong *population we* sort of <u>*go*</u> to work go back home and you know take uhm uhm you know city buses. (ICE-HK:S1B-047#123:1:A)

d. plural verb form for feelings experienced by individuals:
Today Sir I and my colleagues in this ad hoc *group are* <u>glad</u> to present this bill which is the first piece of legislation in Hong Kong. (ICE-HK:S1B-058#78:1:J)

e. singular verb form for mental activities that apply to the whole group:
After failing to resolve their differences, the Hong Kong Cycling *Association has* <u>decided</u> to withdraw all five members from competing in Barcelona. (ICE-HK:S2B-009#87:1:B)

f. singular verb form for expressing unity:
Even if the Preparatory *Committee <u>includes</u>* a numbers of new members with different opinions, it is unlikely that it can stray very much from the recommendations of the PWC. (ICE-HK:S2B-028#102:2:A)

g. plural verb form for signalling diversity:
Their consultancy *staff <u>come</u>* <u>from a wide range of</u> science and business backgrounds, and they take an integral integrated approach to cater to the needs of their clients. (ICE-HK:S2B-042#118:3:A)

h. plural verb form for mention of body parts:
The medical *staff have* their nose to the grindstone seeing and treating patients. (ukspok/04)[1]

Nevertheless, counterexamples abound as far as all these semantic sub-categories of the verb phrase in agreement with collective nouns are concerned, as given in examples (35a–h). Where there are some semantic motivations that emanate from the semantic class of a verb for a singular or plural form to be combined with a collective noun, corpus data from ICE-HK defy such a semantic connection. Hence, when it comes to accounting for concord patterns with collective nouns, it would be 'misleading to say that the verb form is semantically or pragmatically motivated' (Depraetere 2003, p. 124).

(35) a. plural verb form for physical attributes/states of groups
The *audience are* become more sophisticated and our film have to serve up and not down to them. (ICE-HK:S2B-033#14:1:A)
b. plural verb form for involuntary processes undergone by groups
Although some minor amendments have been added to the code over the intervening years, the *majority* of the requirements *have* not been updated since its first publication. (ICE-HK:W2A-039#26:1)
c. singular verb form for physical activities performed by individuals
The Hong Kong Tourist *Association is* organising a familiarisation trip for the captioned group during 5–8 July 1994. (ICE-HK:W1B-028#229:12)
d. singular verb form for feelings experienced by individuals
Mr Patten has called the package a generous and prudent one, but the main political parties have reservations and the expatriate *community is* uneasy about paying into something from which *it* might not benefit. (ICE-HK:S1B-044#X5:1:Z)
e. plural verb form for mental activities that apply to the whole group

---

[1] No example of a plural verb in combination with a typically plural bodily noun phrase can be found in ICE-HK. Consequently, one of Depraetere's (2003, p. 118) examples is reproduced for illustrative purposes. Note also that the abbreviation *ukspok* stands for 'UK spoken'.

The *association* *believe* that Netherlands will benefit from the possibility that patient can request euthanasia from doctors in situation of hopeless and unbearable suffering. (ICE-HK:S2B-030#75:2:A)

f. plural verb form for expressing unity

Church is a place where a *group* of believers *gather* together to carry out the regular religious ceremonials. (ICE-HK:W1A-007#13:1)

g. singular verb form for signalling diversity

In addition, the dolphin *population is* also distributed throughout the Pearl River Estuary to the west of the Hong Kong border. (ICE-HK: W2B-027#15:1)

h. singular verb form for mention of body parts

The Middle East is imploding and the world *community is* sitting on its hands. (ICE-HK:W2E-001#60:4)

3.3.3 Variation Between Native and Non-Native Varieties of English

Both British and American English have been proved to exhibit different preferences for singular/plural concord patterns (Quirk et al. 1985, pp. 16–17; Biber et al. 1999, p. 188; Trudgill and Hannah 2002, p. 70). While plural concord is predominantly used in British English, American English uses singular concord compared with other varieties of English. It appears that American English plays a key role in setting the norms for concord pattern for other world Englishes (Depraetere 2003, pp. 112–113). In HKE, the corpus data on concord pattern preferences clearly exhibit convergence towards the globally dominant American model in that about 80 % of collective nouns in ICE-HK take singular concord, slightly higher than the percentage for British English (see Fig. 3.1). From a linguistic point of view the use of the singular is in any case motivated because it is based on the principle of formal agreement. From a cognitive point of view, a system in which the singular is always used can be less demanding on the speaker's processing effort. However, this preference is somewhat surprising given that British English is the historical input variety and it has influenced some major areas of the society for example, education, judiciary and government

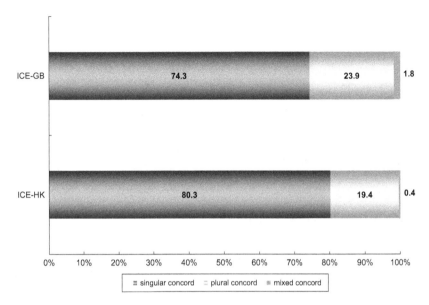

Fig. 3.1 A comparative analysis of different types of concord pattern of collective nouns in ICE-GB and ICE-HK

administration (Bilbow and Li 2001). Judging from the concord pattern preferences revealed from the present study, there appear to be some traces of Americanisation at least in the use of collective nouns in HKE. Equally importantly, the divergence from the British English model documented here could also be taken as evidence that HKE is evolving into a new indigenised variety of English in its own right.

3.3.4 A Note on the Substrate Language Cantonese

Cantonese does not have collective nouns. However, there is a subset of classifiers that are called 'collective classifiers', which 'resemble English collective nouns' (Matthews and Yip 2011, p. 114). For example, the Cantonese classifier *baan1* denotes a 'group', 'bunch' or 'gang' of people, whereas another classifier *cau1* implies a group of objects linked together.

(36) a. *li1 baan1 hok6saang1* 'this class of students'
     b. *gei2 cau1 tai4zi2* 'a few bunches of grapes'
     (Matthews and Yip, 2011, pp. 114–115)

Note that in the two examples above, the head noun is in singular form and thus the sense of collectivity is entirely implied by the use of collective classifiers. Additionally, the issue of concord is irrelevant in Cantonese as it does not have any subject-verb agreement due to the typological differences between English and Chinese in general.

3.4   Concluding Remarks

For the outer-circle and expanding-circle varieties[2]—HKE included—it has been demonstrated that an unambiguously singular subject does not always agree with the third-singular ending of the following verb (Li and Chan 1999, p. 80; Kachru and Nelson 2006, p. 170). This is especially problematic for Hong Kong speakers of English as verbs and nouns do not inflect for number in Chinese (Li and Thompson 1990). By presenting a quantitative and qualitative analysis of singular collective nouns and their subject-verb agreement patterns, this chapter demonstrates important implications in this area. This study has shown that (1) authentic language data provided in the ICE-HK corpus do not support the commonly held 'individuals vs groups' principle for a plural vs. singular form in concord patterns; and (2) the use of a singular/plural verb form to combine with a collective noun is not motivated by the semantics of the verb phrase either. Rather, the study demonstrates that concord variations are strongly governed by convention: individual collective nouns tend to have their own preferences for a singular/plural concord pattern. Singular concord, however, appears to be the preferred choice in HKE. On that note, it

---

[2] In Kachru's (1985, 1992) concentric-circles model for English as a global language, the *inner-circle* of English is made up of countries where English is a native language (e.g. UK) ; the *outer-circle* of English contains those countries (e.g. India, Nigeria, Malaysia) where English is a post-colonial second language; the *expanding circle* is made up of those countries (e.g. China, Indonesia, Nepal) where English is a foreign language. As Melchers and Shaw (2003, p. 169) remark, 'Hong Kong English is somewhat closer to a foreign-language variety than the Malaysian/Singapore variety.'

would be worth mentioning the advice offered by Depraetere (2003, p. 124) that 'it may be safe to advise students to use the singular as the default form, unless there are very clear semantic and/or pragmatic indications that impose the use of a plural verb.' This suggestion certainly holds true for HKE.

References

Aremo, W.B. 2005. On Some Uses of Singular Collective Nouns. *English Today* 21(1): 32–55.

Bache, Carl, and Niels Davidsen-Nielsen. 1997. *Mastering English: An Advanced Grammar for Non-Native and Native Speakers*. Berlin and New York: Mouton de Gruyter.

Bauer, Laurie. 2002. *An Introduction to International Varieties of English*. Edinburgh: Edinburgh University Press.

Biber, Douglas, Susan Conrad, and Geoffrey Leech. 2002. *Longman Student Grammar of Spoken and Written English*. Harlow, UK: Longman.

Biber, Douglas, Stig Johansson, Geoffrey Leech, Susan Conrad, and Edward Finegan. 1999. *Longman Grammar of Spoken and Written English*. Harlow, UK: Longman.

Bilbow, Grahame, and Lan Li. 2001. Following Landscape . . .. *English Today* 17 (4): 27–34.

Collins Cobuild English Grammar. 1990. London: HarperCollins.

Dekeyser, Xavier, Betty Devriendt, Guy A.J. Tops, and Steven Geukens. 1999. *Foundations of English Grammar*. 5th ed. Leuven and Amersfoort: Acco.

Depraetere, Ilse. 2003. On Verbal Concord with Collective Nouns in British English. *English Language and Linguistics* 7(1): 85–127.

Greenbaum, Sidney. 1996. *Oxford English Grammar*. Oxford: Oxford University Press.

Huddleston, Rodney. 1988. *English Grammar: An Outline*. Cambridge: Cambridge University Press.

Huddleston, Rodney, and Geoffrey Pullum. 2002. *The Cambridge Grammar of the English Language*. Cambridge: Cambridge University Press.

Hundt, Marianne. 2006. The Committee Has/Have Decided . . . on Concord Patterns with Collective Nouns in Inner- and Outer-Circle Varieties of English. *Journal of English Linguistics* 34(3): 206–232.

Kachru, Braj. 1985. Standards, Codification and Sociolinguistic Realism: The English Language in the Outer Circle. In *English in the World: Teaching and Learning the Language and Literatures*, ed. Randolph Quirk and Henry Widdowson, 11–36. Cambridge: Cambridge University Press.

———. 1992. World Englishes: Approaches, Issues and Resources. *Language Teaching* 25(1): 1–14.

Kachru, Yamuna, and Cecil Nelson. 2006. *World Englishes in Asian Contexts*. Hong Kong: Hong Kong University Press.

Leech, Geoffrey, and Jan Svartvik. 1994. *A Communicative Grammar of English*. 2nd ed. London and New York: Longman.

Levin, Magnus. 2001. *Agreement with Collective Nouns in English*. (Lund Studies in English, 103). Lund, Sweden: Lund University.

Li, Charles, and Sandra Thompson. 1990. Chinese. In *The Major Languages of East and South-East Asia*, ed. Bernard Comrie, 2nd ed., 83–105. London: Routledge.

Li, David C.S., and Alice Y.W. Chan. 1999. Helping Teachers Correct Structural and Lexical English Errors. *Hong Kong Journal of Applied Linguistics* 4(1): 79–101.

Matthews, Stephen, and Virginia Yip. 2011. *Cantonese: A Comprehensive Grammar*. 2nd ed. London and New York: Routledge.

Melchers, Gunnel, and Philip Shaw. 2003. *World Englishes: An Introduction*. London: Arnold.

Quirk, Randolph, Sidney Greenbaum, Geoffrey Leech, and Jan Svartvik. 1985. *A Comprehensive Grammar of the English Language*. London: Longman.

Swan, Michael. 1995. *Practical English Usage*. 2nd ed. Oxford: Oxford University Press.

Trudgill, Peter, and Jean Hannah. 2002. *International English: A Guide to the Varieties of Standard English*. 4th ed. London: Arnold.

Part II

Discourse

4

Expressions of Gratitude

Abstract Looking at data taken from the ICE-HK corpus, Wong focusses on the use of expressions of gratitude such as *thanks a lot* and *thank you very much* in Hong Kong English. She suggests that Hong Kong speakers of English do not employ a wide variety of thanking strategies and their expressions of gratitude are usually brief, with *thanks* and *thank you* being the most commonly used forms. More often than not, these expressions are used as a closing signal and as a complete turn. Repetitive gratitude formulae and appreciation of the interlocutors in conversations are exceedingly rare, hinting at the possibility of substrate influence that Chinese people in general are being too reserved to express their gratitude openly and explicitly.

Keywords Gratitude expressions • Speech acts • Cross-cultural communication • Formulaic sequences • Hong Kong English

© The Author(s) 2017   **73**
M. Wong, *Hong Kong English*,
DOI 10.1057/978-1-137-51964-1_4

4.1   Introduction

This chapter focusses on the use of expressions of gratitude in spoken discourse and presents results derived from the data from the ICE-HK corpus. Whereas previous studies of thanking expressions have dealt with issues relating to a repertoire of conversational routines of expressing gratitude, this present study confines itself to the analysis of expressions of gratitude containing the stem 'thank', and also includes a discussion of methodological issues. Such issues include, first, the traditional way of studying expressions of gratitude in (inter-language) pragmatic research, and, second, the corpus linguistic analytic approach adopted in this study. A key argument here is that the corpus-linguistic methodology used in such studies has an important effect on uncovering salient pragmatic patterns in the use of expressions of gratitude.

4.2   Previous Research

A substantial amount of previous research has been carried out on the analysis of expressions of gratitude in informal, everyday speech. These expressions are traditionally seen as speech acts and politeness markers. Searle (1969, p. 67) regards *thanks* (*for*) as an illocutionary force indicating device (IFID) that is specified by a set of rules (1969, p. 63):

Propositional content rule: past act A done by H (hearer)
Preparatory rule: A benefits S (speaker) and S believes A benefits S
Sincerity rule: S feels grateful or appreciative for A
Essential rule: counts as an expression of gratitude or appreciation

In Holmes (1984, p. 346), the expression *thank you* is considered a positively affective speech act that can be boosted (e.g. *thank you very much*), as opposed to a negatively affective speech act that can only be mitigated (e.g. **thank you a little*). Leech (1983, p. 84) puts thanking under the 'convivial' category of speech acts, that is, a speech act that is intrinsically polite or courteous.

In present-day English, there are several contexts where thanking is required in order to meet the demands of politeness. In Aijmer's (1996, p. 68) study, these contexts, or types of 'benefaction', are grouped into two broad categories, *material* and *immaterial things*, in the London-Lund corpus.[1] It is interesting to note that Aijmer has 131 examples of 'thanking for a proposal to do something' out of 199 in her 'immaterial' category (65.8 %). Since this context may include such things as a proposal to end a conversation (i.e. a closing signal), the function of thanking goes well beyond expressing gratitude; it can be seen as an element organising the discourse. I will return to this issue in Sect. 4.4.

Aijmer (1996, p. 46) also distinguishes between simple and intensified *thanks/thank you*. The intensified thanking expressions occur in nearly half of her examples (intensified *thanks*: 53.5 %; intensified *thank you*: 40.7 %). The act of thanking is typically boosted by intensifying adverbs for example, *thanks/thank you very much (indeed), thank you so much, thanks awfully, thanks a lot*. Thanking can also be intensified with what Aijmer calls 'compound thanks': 'combinations of different [thanking] strategies' (1996, p. 48). For instance, speakers can express appreciation of the addressee (e.g. *thank you, that's nice of you*), or they can express appreciation of the act (e.g. *thank you, that's lovely*). Each of these strategies can be combined with each other and the gratitude expression itself to create an almost infinite number of thanking forms. In Aijmer's corpus data, 12.8 % of her thanking expressions contain combinations of thanking strategies, with the most frequent combination being *thanks/thank you* and appreciation of the act.

Much of the other research on this topic has been evidently motivated by the need to teach English language learners in a 'second-language' (ESL) or 'foreign-language' (EFL) environment (e.g. Eisenstein and Bodman, 1986; Han 1992; Hinkel 1994; Yates 2004; Diaz Perez 2005), while some other research has also been carried out in the context of other languages such as Japanese (Kimura 1994; Ide 1998;

---

[1] *Material* things are, for example, gifts, hospitality, services, visiting whereas *immaterial* things comprise: compliments, congratulations, well-wishes, interest in one's health, carrying out a request, offer, promise, suggestion, invitation, information, a proposal to do something (e.g. close the conversation).

Kumatoridani 1999). In the former, a cross-cultural perspective is typically adopted to underscore the challenges faced by native and non-native speakers to express thanking adequately to each other. Coulmas (1981) posits that thanking entails indebtedness to the addressee in Japanese culture while it does not in European culture. It is well documented in the literature that Japanese speakers have particular difficulty in English with those expressions of gratitude that imply indebtedness (e.g. Beebe and Takahashi 1989); they tend to confuse 'thank you' with 'I'm sorry', both of which are encoded with the same lexical item in their native language. According to Thomas (1983), misunderstandings could arise not only from language limitations (pragmalinguistic failure) but also from learners' ignorance of social conventions and values in the target language (sociopragmatic failure). In their study of how ESL learners express gratitude in English in some contrived scenarios, Eisenstein and Bodman (1993) note that non-native speakers usually lack the warm and sincere tone conveyed by native speakers; neither do they express reciprocity that native speakers give nor convey it in an appropriate manner. They conclude that expressing gratitude involves 'a complex series of interactions and encodes cultural values and customs' (1993, p. 74).

Of most relevance to the current research is Cheng's (2006) cross-sectional study of inter-language pragmatic development of expressions of gratitude among three groups of Chinese learners of American English (according to their length of stay in the USA). This account, which is based on elicited data from eight predetermined 'thanking' situations set out in a questionnaire distributed to a total of 152 subjects, reveals that (1) Chinese learners and English native speakers have difference preferences for thanking strategies in the eight situations; (2) the length of residence in an English-speaking country (in this case, the USA) has a positive effect on Chinese learners' pragmatic development, as evidenced in their more frequent use of nativelike thanking strategies; (3) Chinese learners' ways of thanking show traces of pragmatic influence from their first language. While Cheng's study is yet another useful contribution to the differences between L1 ('English as a first language') and L2 ('English as a second language') strategies in expressing gratitude, it highlights a major methodological issue that the methodological design of such pragmatic studies has an important effect on determining validity of the results, as will be discussed in the following section.

4.3   Methodological Issues: DCT vs. Corpus Data

Studies focussing on expressions of gratitude have predominantly been based on data elicited from a discourse completion task (DCT), with few exceptions (Bodman and Eisenstein, 1988; Aijmer 1996; Schauer and Adolphs 2006) that use naturally occurring data. The DCT was first used by Blum-Kulka (1982) to examine pragmatic speech act realisations. Since then it has frequently been used as an instrument for the study of inter-language pragmatics. Generally speaking, the aim of the DCT is to investigate a linguistic act within highly predefined parameters such as speaker relationship, language proficiency and nationality of the subjects. The use of a DCT allows researchers to examine what speakers would say in specific contexts that are controlled for a range of factors, such as the relationship to other interlocutors, or the imposition on the interlocutor for which the gratitude is expressed. Although DCTs are one of the most popular instruments in inter-language pragmatics, they have also been criticised for being highly controlled and unnatural (Bardovi-Harlig and Hartford 1993; Yuan 2001; Golato 2003). Schauer and Adolphs (2006) make a strong case for the weaknesses of the DCT approach in their study of expressions of gratitude. Not only does DCT data fail to provide the same variety of linguistic elements, such as laughs, pauses, false starts and hesitations that can be observed in naturally occurring data, it differs from corpus data in participants' preference for certain thanking strategies. Schauer and Adolphs (2006, p. 127ff) discovered that some formulaic sequences that express gratitude for example: 'thanking + confirming interlocutor's commitment' (e.g. *are you sure? Okay, thanks*); 'thanking + stating intent to reciprocate' (e.g. *thanks very much I'll get it next time*); 'thanking + stating interlocutor's non-existent obligation' (e.g. *thank you, but you shouldn't have*) do not appear in their corpus data, although they are used by the native speakers in DCT scenarios.

This is interesting, since these formulaic sequences were also observed by Eisenstein and Bodman (1986, 1993) in their DCT data and in role-plays and by Bodman and Eisenstein (1988) in their field notes taken of naturally occurring data. As Schauer and Adolphs (2006, p. 129) note, 'this discrepancy may be due to the fact that the participants in the discourse completion task had more time to think about their response and have therefore opted to produce an additional politeness strategy'. Another issue that can only be covered in their corpus results is the use of expressions of gratitude over several conversational turns, notably in a service encounter as illustrated below (2006, p. 130).

(Example 1) <S1> Yeah. <SE> laughs </SE> Thank you.
              <S2> Thank you.
              <S1> That's lovely.
              <S2> All right. And your balance is sixty nine thirty six then.
              <S1> Right. <SE> pause </SE> Thank you. Sixty-nine?
              <S2> Er thirty six.
              <S1> Thirty six. Right.
              <S2> Thank you.

The results of Schauer and Adolphs' investigation thus suggest that the data elicited via a DCT can indeed be complemented by corpus data. It is true that the aim of most corpus linguistic studies is to describe patterns of general language use rather than to analyse individual utterances in a highly controlled context. Apart from facilitating language description, corpora also have a place in the language-teaching context by providing learners with patterns of language use in social interactions some of which are not open to intuition.

   With reference to the methodological concerns identified above, in this study, my data consists of real-life spoken discourse by HKE speakers. The data comprises 300 samples of approximately 2,000 words each, and is part of the Hong Kong component of the International Corpus of English (ICE-HK). Table 4.1 outlines the composition of the spoken section of the ICE-HK corpus (see also Chap. 1, Sect. 1.4).

Table 4.1 Composition of spoken ICE-HK

Dialogue	Monologue
S1A: Private (direct conversations and telephone calls)	S2A: Unscripted (spontaneous commentaries, unscripted speeches, demonstrations, legal presentations)
S1B: Public (class lessons, broadcast discussions, broadcast interviews, parliamentary debates, legal cross-examinations, business transactions)	S2B: Scripted (broadcast news, broadcast talks, non-broadcast talks)

My discussion here will centre on the stem 'thank', which is contained in most frequently used formulaic expressions to convey gratitude such as *thanks, thank you, thanks a lot, thank you very much, thank you so much*, and additional sequences or strategies that express gratitude.[2] Wherever possible, I used functional categories described in the literature to code thanking strategies (e.g. Eisenstein and Bodman 1993; Schauer and Adolphs 2006). However, in some instances I had to either make modifications to existing classification systems or create my own tentative terminology where appropriate descriptors had not been previously identified. For example, I coded the following use of gratitude expression (ICE-HK:S1B-064) as an unclear instance.

(Example 2) <#X199:1:A> uhm Mr Loong can you tell us the reason why the management committee agree with the figure of five thousand put forward by the plaintiff <O> Cantonese translation </O> <&> Recording fast-forwards </&>[3]
<#X200:1:Z> That's because uh at the initial stage
<#X201:1:Z> Sorry at
<#X202:1:Z> At the initial stage
<#X203:1:Z> *Thank you*

---

[2] The expressions of gratitude *thank you* and *thanks* are the most common ones in Early Modern English (Jacobsson, 2002) and present-day English (Aijmer, 1996). In the latter, Aijmer (1996, p. 39) mentions the informal *ta* as a morphological variant of *thank you* (or *thanks*) and Schauer and Adolphs (2006, p. 123) adds *cheers* as a casual synonym for *thanks*. However, these two variants are non-existent in ICE-HK.
[3] The <O> element encloses untranscribed text whereas the <&> element includes editorial comment (Nelson, 2006, p. 6).

> <X204:1:Z> They called for <?> tenants </?> for us they out advertisement in the newspaper and they showed the potential uh <?> tenants </?> <?> tenants </?> that is the uhm something that the contractors to look at the uh damaged areas[4]

In this example, the speaker Z who is being interrogated in a cross-examination in court stutters a bit and needs to restart the utterance. Possibly the speaker might have felt the need to thank the audience for their patience. However, in the absence of a level of annotation in the corpus that marks facial expressions, gestures, for example, any interpretation of this particular instance of gratitude expression remains uncertain.

I also modified existing categorisation schemes to cope with the diversity of corpus data. For instance, while Aijmer (1996) considers 'visiting' as a material thing to be thanked for, I expanded this category to include 'coming', 'joining', 'participating' and 'watching' (there are some corpus examples where TV program hosts thank the audience for watching their programmes). Similarly, the immaterial kind of benefaction—'carrying out a request'—was taken to refer also to the acts of answering a question and elaborating on, or offering clarification to, an earlier point. The categorisation scheme on which the present study is based is summarised in Table 4.2.

The data extracting, coding and sorting was carried out with the help of *WordSmith Tools* version 5 (Scott 2010). This Windows-based corpus exploration package has been widely used by linguists to undertake manual linguistic annotation of concordance data, that is, coding individual concordance lines (examples) retrieved from a corpus for structural, functional, discoursal and other features to uncover typical patterns of use. On the basis of a survey of a number of state-of-the-art corpus-processing programs, Smith et al. (2008) have pointed out at least three merits of the *WordSmith Tools* suite for linguistic analysis.

---

[4] The <?> element marks where the transcription is unclear and uncertain.

Table 4.2 Classification system of thanking strategies, thanking responders and types of benefaction

Thanking strategies:

A. Thanking + alerters (A1: attention getter (e.g. *oh*); A2: title (e.g. *Professor*); A3: name (e.g. *Alice*)

B. Thanking + complimenting interlocutor or positive evaluation of previous speaker's utterance (B1: appreciation of the act; B2: appreciation of the addressee)

C. Thanking + confirming interlocutor's commitment

D. Thanking + refusing

E. Thanking + stating intent to reciprocate

F. Thanking + stating interlocutor's non-existent obligation

G. Thanking + stating reason

H. Thanking as a closing signal

I. Thanking as a responder to an expression of gratitude

J. Thanking as a single expression

K. Thanking as an extended turn

Thanking responders:

R1: minimising the favour (e.g. *that's okay*)

R2: expressing pleasure (e.g. *great pleasure*)

R3: expressing appreciation of the addressee (e.g. *you're welcome*)

Type of benefaction:

Material things:

M1: Gift

M2: Hospitality

M3: Services/help

M4: Visiting/joining/coming/participating/watching

Immaterial things:

N1: compliments, congratulations, well-wishes

N2: interest in one's welfare

N3: carrying out a request (e.g. answer a question, clarify an earlier point)

N4: offer, promise, suggestion, invitation

N5: information

N6: a proposal to do something (e.g. closing the conversation)

N7: unclear

1. The 'Set' function of *WordSmith* allows the user to insert a multiple-letter, mnemonic code in a field adjacent to the concordance text, opening up the possibility of entering multiple levels of annotation (e.g. thanking strategies, thanking responders and types of benefaction).

2. The annotation field can be sorted so that concordance lines sharing a common feature can be grouped together, making recurrent patterns of behaviour more visible and the counting of relevant instances of the feature of interest much easier.
3. The user always has access to the larger context (i.e. the source text) of a concordance line, which is essential for a correct classification of individual instances.

The third point is of particular relevance to the present study because the expression of gratitude often spans over a single turn and speakers' response to a gratitude expression can only be examined in the next turn. The source text is also needed to pin down the exact context in which thanking takes place (e.g. upon receipt of a gift).

4.4   The Present Study

A total of 233 thanking expressions were examined for HKE. Forty-three instances of *thanks/thank you* in ICE-HK were discarded from the initial data extraction, which yielded 276 examples. The first category is grammatical errors:

(Example 3) I would like to *thanks* [sic] the delegate who has attend [sic] the conference <...> (ICE-HK:S2B-050#105:2).

The second set of examples occurs in set phrases and other constructions (in which *thank you* can be analysed as a noun phrase or verb phrase rather than a routine formula) that are not of interest in this chapter:

(Example 4) In a note of *thanks* the Deputy President complimented the Governor <...> (ICE-HK:S2B-006#91:2);
(Example 5) *Thanks* God. (ICE-HK:S1B-074#8:1);
(Example 6) I would like to thank to say *thank you* to all <...> (ICE-HK: S2A-034#4:1);

(Example 7) We just need a *thank you* note pad and then we will delete the rest of those questions. (ICE-HK:S1B-079#847:1);
(Example 8) Well first I have to *thank you* for coming. (ICE-HK:S1A-033#7:1:A)

The third set of examples contains an extended turn where expressions of gratitude can be seen as 'a speech act set' (i.e. a composite; see Eisenstein and Bodman 1986) rather than a single speech act; for example, only one instance of gratitude expression is registered to avoid counting the same category twice (ICE-HK:S1B-072):

(Example 9) <#X1:1:Z> Stan *thanks very much* for coming along with this morning.
<#X2:1:Z> It's great to see you.
<X3:1:Z> *Thank you very much* indeed.

The fourth set of examples is used ironically; in such cases, 'thank you' has the illocutionary force of expressing irritation or anger, rather than expressing gratitude (Eisenstein and Bodman 1986, p. 168):

(Example 10) Look look if if if if you discriminate on me on age fine, *thank you very much* then I go elsewhere. (ICE-HK:S1B-080#102:1);
(Example 11) [a dialogue between the race caller and the host about a horse]
<#59:1:A> Uh don't like him uhh one or two spots around on him uh plenty light enough uh if he didn't have a couple of spots you'd say he looked quite well actually he's got the old cross noseband on him as well to try and keep his mouth shut.
<#60:1:A> uh but I'm not overly taken by him.
<#61:1:A> obviously when he opens his mouth he's not nice.
<#62:1:C> Do they come in your size?
<#63:1:A> Oh no *thank you very much*. (ICE-HK:S2A-011)

4.4.1 Strategies of Thanking and Their Distribution Over Situational Contexts

As can be seen in Table 4.3 and Fig. 4.1 (the log-likelihood (LL) score = 338.81, $p < 0.001$), HKE speakers do not employ a wide variety of thanking strategies investigated in previous literature. Rather, their acts of thanking are often used as a closing signal (28.8 %) and as a single turn (26.6 %).[5] They are at times accompanied by titles and names of other speakers (18.5 %) and associated with the preposition *for* for stating reasons of expressing gratitude (16.7%).

While thanking as a closing signal is quite common in face-to-face conversation and telephone calls as in example (12),[6] it is widespread in broadcast discussions (example 13), legal cross-examinations (example 14), and unprepared speeches for example, questions-and-answers sessions (example 15). These speech situations have one thing in common: they are time-constrained and thus speakers in these contexts have to complete their contribution to the ongoing discussion or debate within a specified time span. Once the time is up or they have finished, they often employ the single lexical item *thank you* as a signal to end the discussion or to give the floor back to their interlocutors, as shown in examples (13–15).

In fact, Hymes (1971) states that 'thank you' is often more of a discourse marker than an expression of gratitude in British English, while the latter function is more common in American English, as Eisenstein and Bodman (1993, p. 65) acknowledge. In this respect, HKE seems to be more akin to British English than American English.

(Example 12) <#X423:1:Z> Okay *thank you very much* being help.
          <#424:1:E> You're welcome.
          <#X425:1:Z> Okay *thank you* bye bye.
          <#426:1:E> Bye bye. (ICE-HK:S1A-079)

---

[5] While it might be difficult to determine whether *thanks/thank you* actually marks gratitude or whether it functions as a discourse marker that signals the end of an encounter or discourse episode (Aijmer, 1996, pp. 52–66), the complexity observed in present-day English is not found in the ICE-HK corpus.

[6] The expression of gratitude used as a closing signal is highlighted by an arrow in the left margin of the examples.

Table 4.3 Thanking strategies in ICE-HK

	ICE-HK	
Thanking strategies	Frequency	%
A. Thanking + alerters	43	18.5
B. Thanking + complimenting interlocutor	7	3.0
C. Thanking + confirming interlocutor's commitment	0	0.0
D. Thanking + refusing	3	1.3
E. Thanking + stating intent to reciprocate	0	0.0
F. Thanking + stating interlocutor's non-existent obligation	0	0.0
G. Thanking + stating reason	39	16.7
H. Thanking as a closing signal	67	28.8
I. Thanking as a responder to an expression of gratitude	5	2.1
J. Thanking as a single turn	62	26.6
K. Thanking as an extended turn	7	3.0
Total:	233	100

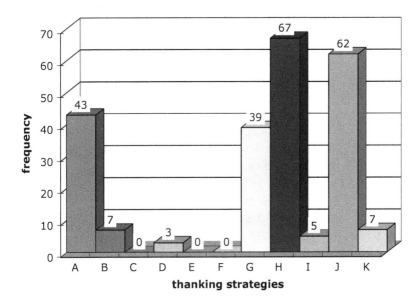

Fig. 4.1   Counts of expressions of gratitude in ICE-HK by strategies

(Example 13) <#X95:1:Z> Well S K uhm that's uh that's all we're
going to have time for this time.
<#X96:1:Z> But I'd like to talk to you again about uh,
your uhm animation project.

<#X97:1:Z> So uh perhaps uh we can talk again in another few weeks, alright?

<#X98:1:Z> *Thanks very much.*

<#99:1:A> Sure.

<#100:1:A> Sure.

<#101:1:A> *Thank you.*[7]

<#102:1:A> Okay. *Thank you* Rhonda.

<#X103:1:Z> S K Fung who is general manager of TVBI. (ICE-HK:S1B-049)

(Example 14) <#97:1:B> The Third Defendant was when he was charged with robbery you were present is that right? <O> Cantonese translation and answer </O>

<#X98:1:Z> Yes.

<99:1:B> There is no further questions *thank you.* (ICE-HK:S1B-069)

(Example 15) <#71:1:A> But my opinion or my view is that uh when <.> Ch </.> China is changing.[8]

<#72:1:A> In fact China <.> i </.> is not many things are uncertain many things are not steady.

<#73:1:A> They are changing almost <.> dai </.> uh from day to day.

<#74:1:A> So uh any system today may be different tomorrow in fact.

<#75:1:A> It's not like uh Hong Kong we are <.> w </.> well established.

<#76:1:A> They are not well established.

<#77:1:A> They are changing.

<#78:1:A> So in the future the way I see it is that uh China accounting education will become more and more uh like Western.

<#79:1:A> There will still be differences but there will be more similarities between uh China and the rest.

<#80:1:A> *Thank you.* (ICE-HK:S2A-023)

---

[7] This expression of gratitude is considered as a responder to the preceding thanking expression uttered by speaker Z.

[8] The <.> tag indicates incomplete words in the original recordings.

Looking at the corpus data I can see that in single expressions of gratitude *thanks* and *thank you* tend to be used as complete turns more frequently than any of the longer formulaic sequences such as *thank you very much* and *thanks a lot*. In fact, the intensified expressions of gratitude are not common, with four instances of *thanks a lot*, twenty-nine cases of *thank you very much*, three occurrences of *thanks very much* and just one example of *thanks indeed*. It is also worth noting that the single lexical items *thanks* and *thank you* are often used in everyday conversation (example 16), and in courts where the lawyer uses the lexical item *thank you* to indicate gratitude for the interlocutors' co-operation in cross-examinations (example 17).

(Example 16) <#273:1:B> Yeah can you bought some CDs for me?
<#X274:1:Z> Oh yeah what do you want?
<#275:1:B> Yah because I'm I'm I'm teaching in uhm teaching ballet in a school but uhm since uhm Hong Kong the Hong Kong uh Records does not uh contain any uh CDs about uhm ballet music I would like to buy some.
<#276:1:A> Yeah.
<#X277:1:Z> Oh yeah yeah definitely.
<#278:1:B> Yah *thank you.*
<#X279:1:Z> Welcome. (ICE-HK:S1A-055)

(Example 17) <#X167:2:Z> And as described in the police submission form it was a bed sheet seized from the bed on which AP two raped the victim.
<#168:2:A> I see.
<#169:2:A> And can you tell which from which area of the bed sheet that you have this <.> hu </.> human spermatozoa?
<#X170:2:Z> Well it's very difficult to particularly name an area on a bed sheet because you would understand and I'd be appreciate that there is no particular reference but I have made a drawing here uh if you would allow me okay it is this is the bed sheet as laid out and it's on here okay.
</X>
<#171:2:A> Yes.

<#X172:2:Z> I mean.
<#X173:2:Z> Yes we can see that.
<#174:2:A> *Thank you.* (ICE-HK:S1B-069)

One-fifth of the ICE-HK corpus data contains thanking expressions followed by other speakers' titles and names. The former is particularly frequent in parliament debates where interlocutors are often addressed by the role they play in the parliament, whereas the latter is frequently used in spontaneous commentaries (notably horse racing) in which first names are used by the host to refer to the commentators. Both of these names and titles are uttered along with expressions of gratitude, as in examples (18) and (19).

(Example 18)   <#35:1:A> I'm the captain Steve Mooney.
<#36:1:A> We will be joined later on by Franko Lau.
<#37:1:A> quickly loading though for the second race and our race caller for this evening is none other than Harry Troy.
<#38:1:B> *Thanks Steve* and we've just got one other runner to go forward and make the line complete. (ICE-HK:S2A-020)

(Example 19)   <#X118:1:Z> I will allow two more questions on that.
<#X119:1:Z> Ms Emily Lau.
<#120:1:A> Uh *thank you Chairman.*
<#121:1:A> Chairman I want to ask the Foreign Secretary about uh a question on uh violations of human rights after nineteen ninety-seven. (ICE-HK:S1B-051)

A further one-fifth of corpus data accounts for the 'thanking + stating reason' strategy. Expressions of gratitude in this category typically begin with *thanks/thank you* and are then followed by verb + *ing*, as shown in example (20). The majority of the expressions in the category are used in broadcast news in which the host thanks the audience for watching the news program, as illustrated in examples (21) and (22).

(Example 20) <#32:2:A> Will be expecting the demo uhm but it will come only after my let say fifteen minutes of uh brief introduction about the concept of creating the Winword two point o.

<#33:2:A> Uh once again *thank you for coming here and spending time with us.* (ICE-HK:S2A-022)

(Example 21) <#118:2:B> Good evening.

<#119:2:B> *Thanks for joining us.*

<#120:2:B> The Financial Secretary projects an extra five billion dollars could be spent on public services in next year's budget.

<#121:2:B> Hamish Macleod announced the windfall today in his unprecedented budget consultations with Legislators. (ICE-HK:S2B-009)

(Example 22) <#71:1:Z> That's the main news.

<#72:1:Z> *Thanks for watching.*

<#73:1:Z> Good night. (ICE-HK:S2B-004)

In expressing their gratitude, HKE speakers seldom (3 %) compliment the interlocutors (see example 23), nor repeat sequences and lexical items of gratitude in an extended turn (see example 24). One possible explanation for the rarity of these strategies in ICE-HK might be that the use of these thanking strategies depends very much on the specific situational conditions and the interlocutors' relationship that might not be covered very well in the corpus. Another possible explanation would be that Chinese people are being too reserved to express their gratitude openly and explicitly. By contrast, these 'gratitude clusters' are commonplace in other cultures (Schauer and Adolphs 2006, p. 126). Cheng (2006, p. 16) remarks that the Chinese people seldom verbalise their gratitude, particularly with intimate family members. This might perhaps reflect the lack of cultural congruity between Chinese and western culture and echo what Eisenstein and Bodman have proposed, which is that expressing gratitude has important social value:

> Used frequently in a wide range of interpersonal relationships, this function, when appropriately expressed, can engender feelings of warmth and

solidarity among interlocutors. Conversely, the failure to express gratitude adequately can have negative consequences for the relationship of speaker and listener. (1993, p. 64)

HKE speakers who are unaware of the underlying rules for expressing gratitude in English might find it very difficult to perform the expression of gratitude successfully. Therefore, Sect. 4.5 will be devoted to how this function of expressing gratitude can be performed more effectively in everyday communication.

(Example 23) <#681:1:A> Okay maybe I buy you a lunch.
             <#X682:1:Z> *Oh thank you.*
             <#X683:1:Z> *That's very sweet of you.* (ICE-HK:S1A-067)
(Example 24) <#685:1:A> *Thank you for helping me for in this assignment.*
             <#686:1:A> *And thank you really thank you.*
             <#X687:1:Z> Oh it's -
             <#X688:1:Z> You're welcome. (ICE-HK:S1A-067)

In addition, I can hardly find instances of *thanks/thank you* being used as a responder to an expression of gratitude. As Schauer and Adolphs (2006, p. 126) note, an expression of gratitude is not commonly mentioned in typical textbook conversations as a possible responder to the preceding thanking act. That might be the reason why HKE speakers rarely employ *thank you* as a response to their interlocutors' expressions of gratitude, as in example (25).[9] The issue of responding to thanking expressions will be taken up in the following sub-section.

(Example 25) <#X97:1:Z> So uh perhaps uh we can talk again in another few weeks, alright?
             <#X98:1:Z> *Thanks very much.*
             <#99:1:A> Sure.
             <#100:1:A> Sure.
             <#101:1:A> *Thank you.* (ICE-HK:S1B-049)

---

[9] A more complete version of the dialogue is presented in example (13).

Furthermore, category D: 'thanking + refusing' is also rare in ICE-HK. Knowing the right words to politely reject an offer is essential in every language. Unfortunately, the ICE-HK data only contains three instances (1 %) for this important strategy (see example 26). These results might seem to suggest that Hong Kong people (and the Chinese in general) are not inclined to refuse an offer. More research is however needed to verify this claim. On the other hand, this finding seems to lend support to Schauer and Adolphs' (2006, p. 129) suggestion that 'the ability to express gratitude and at the same time to refuse a proposition is one of the main skills that students may need to possess in a native speaker context'. HKE speakers might simply lack the words for expressing themselves more fully and rejecting more appropriately rather than feeling embarrassed to do so.

(Example 26)   <#X632:1:Z> I've got to phone home cos I think it's my flatmate birthday today I've to ring her.
          <#633:1:B> Birthday.
          <#634:1:A> If if it's birthday today,
          <#X635:1:Z> Not really know yah I think so.
          <#636:1:A> A call do you want to call her?
          <#X637:1:Z> *No thanks.*
          <#X638:1:Z> *No no no no no I'll do it anyway thanks.*
          (ICE-HK:S1A-030)

There are no examples of the structures such as 'thanking + confirming interlocutor's commitment', 'thanking + stating intent to reciprocate' and 'thanking + stating interlocutor's non-existent obligation' (see Sect. 4.3 for examples). This finding is not entirely surprising as there is no evidence either in real-life spoken data of British English (e.g. Aijmer 1996; Schauer and Adolphs 2006). In fact, these areas have been highlighted by Schauer and Adolphs (2006, p. 129) as particularly problematic in their comparison of DCT and corpus data with respect to expressions of gratitude. They are regarded as 'an additional politeness strategy', which participants in the discourse completion task opted to produce as they have more time to plan the utterance. In naturally occurring discourse however, these strategies might not at all be possible as the nature of the discourse requires much faster processing of information and speech. According to Coulmas (1981), thanking and responding to being thanked are reactive speech acts; speakers have to react to an act of thanking quickly. These thanking strategies might even be tough for HKE speakers when they need to express their gratitude in a language that is not their native tongue.

4.4.2 Responders to Gratitude Expressions

A gratitude expression can be followed by a 'responder'. Aijmer (1996, p. 40) notes several instances of thanking responders in present-day British English; these are *that's okay* (minimising the favour), *great pleasure* (expressing pleasure) and *you're welcome* (expressing appreciation of the addressee). As shown in Table 4.4,[10] just 18 out 233 expressions of gratitude are responded to in the Hong Kong corpus data. In other words, one in every thirteen occurrences of thanking is followed by a responder in the ICE-HK. Although the figures presented here are rather small for ICE-HK and any concrete conclusion should therefore be avoided, it seems that it is uncommon for HKE speakers to contribute to the continuation of a thanking act by responding to it appropriately.

Apart from a low frequency of thanking responders, HKE has also exhibited a rather limited range of responders. None of the thanking responders found in ICE-HK is used to express pleasure (R2). Responders used to minimise the favour (R1) are restricted to a few common discourse elements such as *all right*, *okay* and *yeah*, as in examples (27–29).

(Example 27) <#244:1:B> He's a smart guy right.
<#245:1:A> I don't know.
<#246:1:A> Oh Cindy *thanks so much* <O> laughter </O>
<#247:1:B> **All right that's that's all right**. (ICE-HK: S1A-098)

---

[10] No statistical test of significance can be carried out due to the very small frequencies.

Table 4.4 Thanking responders in ICE-HK

	ICE-HK	
Thanking responders	Frequency	%
R1: minimising the favour	7	38.9
R2: expressing pleasure	0	0.0
R3: expressing appreciation of the addressee	11	61.1
Total:	18	100.0

(Example 28) <#X321:1:Z> And what did the customer say it's good about our shop?
<#322:1:C> Uhm.
<#323:1:C> The staffs are nice.
<#X324:1:Z> Okay *thank you very much*. Well done.
<#325:1:C> **Okay**. (ICE-HK:S1A-079)
(Example 29) <#X66:1:Z> We pay much more than we should.
<#67:1:A> Yeah there's no <?> with </?> discount and not quite reasonable.
<#68:1:A> So so yeah the best thing you can get is from travel agency.
<#69:1:A> And I have ask my cousin's boyfriend.
<#70:1:A> I have just ring.
<#71:1:A> He hasn't relied.
<#X72:1:Z> It's not fair.
<#X73:1:Z> Really.
<#X74:1:Z> Okay cool *thanks*.
<#X75:1:Z> *Thanks a lot*.
<#76:1:A> **Yeah**. (ICE-HK:S1A-089)

The responder *you're welcome* is used exclusively to express appreciation of the addressee who performs the thanking act (R3; see examples 30–32), possibly as a result of didactic teaching the formulaic sequence *you're welcome* is seen as a 'proper' response to an expression of gratitude in nearly every context.

(Example 30) <#X7:1:Z> Yah and I I don't know where else in Hong Kong where I can book tennis court.
<#X8:1:Z> I was told that the public court is very hard to book.
<#9:1:A> Uhm
<#10:1:A> Yah.
<#11:1:B> Yeah yeah yeah.
<#12:1:A> Uhm.
<#13:1:A> Oh I I can uh help you to ask, yah.
<X14:1:Z> Okay okay that would be great *thanks*.
<#15:1:A> **You're welcome**. (ICE-HK:S1A-010)

(Example 31) <#X2:1:Z> Television Broadcast it <?> in </?> known to us as TVB has uh an associated company TVBI and uh the
<#X3:1:Z> The job of that company is to sell and uh sell to new markets and uh expand existing market for Chinese language TV programming.
<#X4:1:Z> Uhm the general manager of TVBI is S K Fung.
<#X5:1:Z> And I have him on the line now.
<#X6:1:Z> Hello S K.
<#7:1:A> Hello Rhonda.
<#8:1:A> How are you?
<#9:1:A> Good evening.
<#X10:1:Z> I'm
<#X11:1:Z> I'm good.
<#X12:1:Z> *Thanks for for joining us*.
<#13:1:A> **You're welcome**. (ICE-HK:S1B-049)

(Example 32) <#X364:1:Z> Yeah I need your help.
<#X365:1:Z> You never know.
<#366:1:A> All right I'm I will always stand by you and give you my help if I can.
<#X367:1:Z> Wow.
<#X368:1:Z> *Thank you*.
<#X369:1:Z> *Thank you very much*.
<#370:1:A> **You're welcome**. <&> laughter </&>
(ICE-HK:S1A-035)

4.4.3 Implications for Cross-Cultural Communication and Language Proficiency

While research studies on World Englishes are largely set apart from those on second/foreign language acquisition and given the fact that new varietal features are never considered as learner errors, the current object of study can provide a bridge between these two research paradigms (see Mukherjee and Hundt 2011 for the pioneering work on this connection), since expression of gratitude is not so much purely an issue of 'what is being said' in different varieties of English but 'what is being communicated' in social interactions. In fact, words used to express gratitude have been classified as socio-interactional formulaic sequences (Nattinger and DeCarrico 1992; Wray 2000). Recent research has illustrated the key role of formulaic sequences in the context of cross-cultural communication. As Schmitt and Carter (2004, p. 10) point out, it is important for learners to use formulaic sequences appropriately in their conversations with native speakers since 'interlocutors expect them, and they are the preferred choice. Thus, formulaic sequences are not only useful for efficient language usage; they are essential for appropriate language use'. Thus, as Ellis argues, 'the job of the language learner is to learn these familiar word sequences' based on the assumption that 'speaking natively is speaking idiomatically using frequent and familiar collocations' (1997, p. 129). With regard to formulaic sequences of gratitude expressions, as early as in Early Modern English, language teaching texts have shown a high incidence of *thank you* and *thanks*, suggesting that 'thanking was considered very important for learners of a language' (Jacobsson 2002, p. 70).

Since formulaic sequences are so important to cross-cultural communication and language proficiency, it seems appropriate that teaching materials should equip language learners with a repertoire of formulaic sequences and expressions of gratitude that allows learners to convey their thanks in an appropriate manner even at a relatively early learning stage. However, in four randomly selected textbooks for beginner and intermediate learners examined by Schauer and Adolphs (2006, p. 122), not only does the number of sequences included in the course books differ considerably the beginner level books did not contain the rather important formulaic sequence of 'thanking + stating reason'. Bodman and Eisenstein's (1988) and Eisenstein and Bodman's (1993) investigations further show that even advanced learners display difficulties in choosing formulaic replies when expressing their gratitude. As they argue, the advanced learners of English 'need information on the nature of what to say, the language used to express it, and the context in which it is needed' (1993, p. 75).

In contrast to the English that we find in textbooks, which is deficient in correct routines or expressions that are consistently automatized in the native English speaker, some large corpora collected from native speakers of English such as the British National Corpus[11] can provide learners with a much wider variety of formulaic sequences of expressions of gratitude. Such corpora serve as a better basis from which we can derive language-teaching materials than the judgements made about a language by a single author. In addition, corpus data can provide us with information that is not easily accessible by intuition, such as frequency information (see, for example, Sinclair 1991). For instance, the 'thanking + stating reason' and 'thanking + refusing' structures are by far the most commonly used thanking strategies amongst native English speakers in Schauer and Adolphs' (2006, p. 127) corpus-based account. However, my investigation has shown that HKE speakers seldom adopt the latter strategy. The frequency of occurrence of different strategies of expressing gratitude can thus be used as one of the guiding principles for the selection and prioritising of language content that is, sequencing in ELT materials (e.g. Leech 2001) with regard to the teaching of formulaic sequences. More focus can be given to teaching the ways in which one can express gratitude and at the same time refuse an offer. Another issue that can be covered in the teaching of gratitude expressions is the predominance of extended turns used to express gratitude in native-speaking environments, which is again lacking in my data. Some awareness-raising activities can therefore be devoted to learning additional sequences or lexical items that express gratitude across turns.

---

[11] http://www.natcorp.ox.ac.uk/ (accessed 5 January 2017).

4.5 Concluding Remarks: Some Insights into Substrate Influence and Cross-Cultural Differences in Language Values and Customs

Cross-cultural differences are closely tied to the traditional Chinese way of thinking. Eisenstein and Bodman note that different cultures have shown 'significant differences between the ways in which gratitude was expressed' (1986, p. 170). For example, as high value is placed on modesty and humility in Chinese culture, in response to an offer of a pay rise, a Chinese speaker would most probably say: 'Thank you very much. But I think I have not done so well to get a raise. Anyway, I'd try to do better' (1993, p. 74). In fact, in many situations where Chinese respond to praise, they prefer routinized denials (e.g. *I'm not*) rather than appreciation tokens (e.g. *Thank you*); such rejections might be considered impolite or even rude from a westerner's viewpoint (Yu 1999). On the other hand, HKE speakers do not seem to have any misinterpretation in this respect when they talk to each other, as in the following example (33; ICE-HK:S1A-027) found in ICE-HK. This example is a testimony to substrate influence from Cantonese (or more generally Chinese) where, as Matthews and Yip (2011, p. 427) point out, there is a general tendency to play down compliments through various strategies such as using a rhetorical question *bin1dou6 hai6 le1* (literally meaing 'where is it [compliment]?' and metaphorically meaning 'I don't think so!') and treating the compliment as an exaggeration for example, *taai3 gwo3zeong2 laa3* (literally meaing 'too over-compliment' and metaphorically meaning 'you're too kind'). To reply to an expression of thanks, Cantonese speakers tend to use *m4sai2* 'no need' (for thanks)' or *m4sai2 haak3hei3* 'no need to be so polite', as in example (33) in which the English negative word *no* is used.

(Example 33) <#X688:2:Z> *Thank you* <&> All speakers laugh </&>
                    <#689:2:A> **No** you're welcome.
                    <#X690:2:Z> **No** thank you.

Other problematic examples investigated by Eisenstein and Bodman of their Chinese subjects include: 'That won't be necessary. Anyway, thank you so much' (in response to an offer of a farewell party); 'It is so glad to me that I have such kind of good friend' (in response to an offer of a US $500 loan from a friend); 'Thank you. Blue is my favourite colour but it is not sad for me' (in response to a gift of a blue sweater; using inappropriate humour) (1986, p. 184). As Eisenstein and Bodman (1993, p. 74) comment, their American subjects find these kinds of utterances difficult to interpret and find them strange, expected, uncomfortable and confusing.

The fact that the Chinese speakers in Eisenstien and Bodman's studies respond 'awkwardly' clearly suggests that they tend to transfer incongruent social rules, values and belief systems from their native language and culture into their speaking English. Hopefully, this chapter has provided some insights into these incongruities. The Hong Kong Chinese tend to be rather reserved in expressing their gratitude explicitly and thus they seldom show appreciation of the interlocutors in their expression of gratitude, nor do they employ an extended turn for thanking. In addition, it is probable that they will express gratitude and reject an offer. As Smith (1987) insightfully points out, an awareness of how speech acts are performed is more essential to cross-cultural communication than an awareness of lexis or syntax.

This study has offered a few glimpses of different aspects of expressing gratitude by HKE speakers and the implications of the way this function can be performed more effectively in social interactions with the help of the corpus findings. Further research can focus on how this function is performed in the native language of Hong Kong people (i.e. Cantonese) in order to arrive at a more accurate analysis of the data.

References

Aijmer, Karin. 1996. *Conversational Routines in English*. London: Longman.
Bardovi-Harlig, Kathleen, and Beverly Hartford. 1993. Learning the Rules of Academic Talk: A Longitudinal Study of Pragmatic Development. *Studies in Second Language Acquisition* 15(3): 279–304.

Beebe, Leslie, and Tomoko Takahashi. 1989. Do You Have a Bag? Social Status and Patterned Variation in Second Language Acquisition. In *Variation in Second Language Acquisition: Discourse and Pragmatics*, ed. Susan Gass, Carolyn Madden, Dennis Preston, and Larry Selinker, 103–125. Clevedon and Philadelphia: Multilingual Matters.

Blum-Kulka, Shoshana. 1982. Learning How to Say What You Mean in a Second Language: A Study of the Speech Act Performance of Learners of Hebrew as a Second Language. *Applied Linguistics* 3(1): 29–59.

Bodman, Jean, and Miriam Eisenstein. 1988. May God Increase Your Bounty: The Expressions of Gratitude in English by Native and Non-Native Speakers. *Cross Currents* 15(1): 1–21.

Cheng, Stephanie Weijung. 2006. A Exploratory Cross-Sectional Study of Interlanguage Pragmatic Development of Expressions of Gratitude by Chinese Learners of English. Unpublished PhD Thesis, University of Iowa, USA.

Coulmas, Florian. 1981. 'Poison to Your Soul': Thanks and Apologies Contrastively Viewed. In *Conversational Routine: Explorations in Standardized Communication Situations and Prepatterned Speech*, ed. Florian Coulmas, 69–91. The Hague: Mouton.

Diaz Perez, Francisco Javier. 2005. The Speech Act of Thanking in English: Differences Between Native and Non-Native Speakers' Behaviour. *ES: Revista de Filologia Inglesa* 26(2005): 91–101.

Eisenstein, Miriam, and Jean Bodman. 1986. 'I Very Appreciate': Expressions of Gratitude by Native and Non-Native Speakers of American English. *Applied Linguistics* 7(2): 167–185.

———. 1993. Expressing Gratitude in American English. In *Interlanguage Pragmatics*, ed. Gabriele Kasper and Shoshana Blum-Kulka, 64–81. Oxford and New York: Oxford University Press.

Ellis, Nick. 1997. Vocabulary Acquisition: Word Structure, Collocation, Word-Class, and Meaning. In *Vocabulary: Description, Acquisition and Pedagogy*, ed. Norbert Schmitt and Michael McCarthy, 122–139. Cambridge: Cambridge University Press.

Golato, Andrea. 2003. Studying Compliment Responses: A Comparison of DCTs and Recordings of Naturally Occurring Talk. *Applied Linguistics* 21(1): 90–121.

Han, Chung-hye. 1992. A Comparative Study of Compliment Responses: Korean Females in Korean Interactions and in English Interactions. *Working Papers in Educational Linguistics* 8(2): 17–31.

Hinkel, Eli. 1994. Pragmatics of Interaction: Expressing Thanks in a Second Language. *Applied Language Learning* 5(1): 73–91.

Holmes, Janet. 1984. Modifying Illocutionary Force. *Journal of Pragmatics* 8(3): 345–365.

Hymes, Dell. 1971. Sociolinguistics and the Ethnography of Speaking. In *Social Anthropology and Language*, ed. Edwin Ardener, 47–93. London: Tavistock.

Ide, Risako. 1998. 'Sorry for Your Kindness': Japanese Interactional Ritual in Public Discourse. *Journal of Pragmatics* 29(5): 509–529.

Jacobsson, Mattias. 2002. *Thank You* and *Thanks* in Early Modern English. *ICAME Journal* 26(2002): 63–80.

Kimura, Kazumi. 1994. The Multiple Functions of *Sumimasen*. *Issues in Applied Linguistics* 5(2): 279–302.

Kumatoridani, Tetsuo. 1999. Alternation and Co-Occurrence in Japanese Thanks. *Journal of Pragmatics* 31(5): 623–642.

Leech, Geoffrey. 1983. *Principles of Pragmatics*. London: Longman.

———. 2001. The Role of Frequency in ELT: New Corpus Evidence Brings a Re-Appraisal. *Foreign Language Teaching and Research* 33(5): 328–339.

Matthews, Stephen, and Virginia Yip. 2011. *Cantonese: A Comprehensive Grammar*. 2nd ed. London and New York: Routledge.

Mukherjee, Joybrato, and Marianne Hundt, eds. 2011. *Exploring Second-Language Varieties of English and Learner Englishes: Bridging a Paradigm Gap*. Amsterdam and Philadelphia: John Benjamins.

Nattinger, James, and Jeanette DeCarrico. 1992. *Lexical Phrases and Language Teaching*. Oxford: Oxford University Press.

Nelson, Gerald. 2006. *The ICE Hong Kong Corpus: User Manual*. London: University College London.

Schauer, Gila, and Svenja Adolphs. 2006. Expressions of Gratitude in Corpus and DCT Data: Vocabulary, Formulaic Sequences, and Pedagogy. *System* 34(1): 119–134.

Schmitt, Norbert, and Ronald Carter. 2004. Formulaic Sequences in Action. In *Formulaic Sequences: Acquisition, Processing and Use*, ed. Norbert Schmitt, 1–22. Amsterdam and Philadelphia: John Benjamins.

Scott, Mike. 2010. Introduction to WordSmith Tools. http://www.lexically.net/downloads/version5/HTML/index.html. Accessed 14 June 2016.

Searle, John. 1969. *Speech Acts: An Essay in the Philosophy of Language*. Cambridge: Cambridge University Press.

Sinclair, John. 1991. *Corpus, Concordance, Collocation*. Oxford: Oxford University Press.

Smith, Larry. 1987. Introduction: Discourse Strategies and Cross-Cultural Communication. In *Discourse Across Cultures: Strategies in World Englishes*, ed. Larry Smith, 1–6. New York: Prentice Hall.

Smith, Nicholas, Sebastian Hoffmann, and Paul Rayson. 2008. Corpus Tools and Methods, Today and Tomorrow: Incorporating Linguists' Manual Annotations. *Literary and Linguistic Computing* 23(2): 163–180.

Thomas, Jenny. 1983. Cross-Cultural Pragmatic Failure. *Applied Linguistics* 4(2): 91–112.

Wray, Alison. 2000. Formulaic Sequences in Second Language Teaching: Principle and Practice. *Applied Linguistics* 21(4): 463–489.

Yates, Lynda. 2004. The 'Secret Rules of Language': Tackling Pragmatics in the Classroom. *Prospect* 19(1): 3–21.

Yu, Ming-chung. 1999. Cross-Cultural and Interlanguage Pragmatics: Developing Communicative Competence in a Second Language. Unpublished PhD Thesis, Harvard University, USA.

Yuan, Yi. 2001. An Inquiry into Empirical Pragmatics Data-Gathering Methods: Written DCTs, Oral DCTs, Field Notes, and Natural Conversation. *Journal of Pragmatics* 33(2): 271–292.

5

Code-Mixing of Indigenous Cantonese Words into English

Abstract Focussing on the code-mixing phenomenon in Hong Kong English, Wong offers a detailed literature review on the ways in which English elements are being mixed into Cantonese and thus she argues that there is far less scholarship on code-mixing of indigenous Cantonese words into English. She also draws attention to the crucial argument that this kind of unexplored code-mixing pattern could be related to ethnic solidarity and identity. Having examined the ICE-HK corpus, she finds out that Cantonese colloquial formulaic sequences and cultural expressions occur prominently in both spoken and written texts, suggesting that code-mixing could be a solidarity marker. The chapter also explores other motivations for code-mixing such as the absence of a semantic match between Cantonese proper nouns and their English translations.

Keywords Code-mixing • Cantonese • Indigenous words • Identity • Hong Kong English

© The Author(s) 2017
M. Wong, *Hong Kong English*,
DOI 10.1057/978-1-137-51964-1_5

5.1   Introduction

This chapter focusses on a case study of pragmatic functions of indigenous formulaic sequences in Hong Kong English (HKE). As forcefully argued in Levinson's (1983, pp. 5–35) seminal introduction on the subject, pragmatics covers a vast range and is thus one of the least clearly defined fields in linguistics (see Ariel 2010 for a more recent and richer description). The areas of analysis range from, traditionally, deixis, speech acts and conversational implicatures, to what Ariel refers to as 'beyond pragmatics' as in work on stance, nonliteral references, interactional patterns and discourse styles (see, Ariel 2010, Chap. 8 and the references therein). The latter broadly defined approach to pragmatics can be found in, for example, Denke's (2009) investigations of pragmatic markers with different subfunctions (e.g. social functions as repair markers and textual functions as discourse markers) in native and non-native oral presentations in Swedish and British universities, as well as in Lin's (2013) analysis of multiword sequences (MWSs) employed in different modes of intercultural communication, serving three central pragmatic functions: managing social interaction; introducing necessary topics and linking utterances; and in corpora of online and spoken discourse. Likewise, discursive MWSs in the 'Comprehensive Method' of categorising MWSs outlined in Erman et al. (2013) are broadly conceived of as 'multi-word pragmatic markers' that in spoken discourse generally convey: a mitigating value (e.g. I was wondering …); an evidential meaning (e.g. I think …); and an interactional function (e.g. don't you think?).

For present purposes, the definition of pragmatics given in Cruse (2004) will be adopted:

> [P]ragmatics can be taken to be concerned with aspects of information (in the widest sense) conveyed through language which (a) are not encoded by generally accepted convention in the linguistic forms used, but which (b) nonetheless arise naturally out of and depend on the meanings conventionally encoded in the linguistic forms used, and taken in conjunction with the context in which the forms are used. (Cruse 2004, p. 14)

As can be seen my approach to pragmatics is a fairly encompassing one, moving well beyond linguistic construal of meanings into domains where lexical resources are deployed to function contextually as signals or markers of group affiliation. My intention is to flag the existence of a wide array of multiword/formulaic sequences (or, in Granger's (1998) terminology, 'pragmatic markers') that are used to negotiate group identity with the help of corpus evidence.

Specifically, the focus of the pragmatic analysis of formulaic sequences will be on the use of mixed codes in Hong Kong. Extensive research on the mixing of English vocabulary into Cantonese has been conducted with anecdotal evidence, speech samples, newspapers and magazines (e.g. Gibbons 1983, 1987; Li 1996; Chan 1998, 2003, 2007; Bauer 2006; Wong et al. 2007). Less common, however, has been the use of code-mixing the other way round—that is, Hong Kong people regularly use indigenous Cantonese words while speaking in English. The use of a single indigenous expression (e.g. *chah chaan teng* 'a type of Hong Kong-style restaurant serving a mixture of Chinese and western food' as in example 1) in largely English-language discourse could provide some hints about the pragmatic motivation of code-mixing in relation to ethnic identity (i.e. Hong Kong Chinese; cf. Martin 2005, p. 120). This chapter, then, seeks to offer a small contribution in this context with the hope of showing that code-mixing is especially tuned to the negotiation of group membership (thus solidarity).

(Example 1) B: It's just like a normal fast food not fast food uhm <indig> *chah chaan teng* </indig> <&> a Cantonese bistro serving Chinese and Chinese-Western food </&> kind of restaurant.[1] (ICE-HK:S1A-100#86)

The remainder of the chapter will provide a qualitative and partly quantitative account of the code-mixing phenomenon in HKE. As outlined in Sect. 5.3, there have been many extensive studies of English elements being mixed into Cantonese in the literature but there is much less

---

[1] The <indig> element encloses an indigenous expression, while the <&> element contains editorial comment, conveying the meaning of the Cantonese expression in English.

information available on the pragmatic functions of code-mixing of indigenous Cantonese words into English. My central argument is that this kind of unexplored code-mixing pattern could serve the pragmatic function of negotiating ethnic solidarity and identity. In Sect. 5.4, some 700 instances of mixed code extracted from the ICE-HK corpus will be briefly discussed in semantic terms. The pragmatic aspects of the mixed code, then, will be dealt with in Sect. 5.5. It will be shown that a high incidence of Cantonese colloquial formulaic sequences and cultural expressions in the spoken and written texts of the corpus tends to suggest that code-mixing is a solidarity marker signalling in-group membership. Another pragmatic motivation for code-mixing, namely, the absence of a semantic match between Cantonese proper nouns and their English translations, will also be considered. Sect. 5.6 concludes the chapter by summarising the findings and offering brief orientations for future research. In the next section (5.2) a sketch of the linguistic landscape in Hong Kong is provided.

5.2   Background on Code Choices in Hong Kong

It is hardly disputed, in Hong Kong, that English is highly regarded by local people as it is the world's most important international language (Crystal 2003) as well as the official language used in government administration, the legislature, the judiciary and higher education. It does not mean, however, that Hong Kong people are hostile towards their native language, Cantonese. For instance, Fu's (1975) attitude survey suggests that the Hong Kong people are loyal to their mother tongue. Nearly two decades later, Pennington and Yue (1994, pp. 10–11) arrive at a similar finding in their research with secondary students: 'students did not feel that use of English threatened their ethnolinguistic identity'. Chinese remains a symbol of ethnic solidarity. As Yau (1993) observes rightly, the two codes are associated with different attitudes or beliefs and serve different pragmatic/discourse purposes: while English is used solely for communication, people use the Cantonese language to express their identity; 'to signal to other people who they are and what group(s) they belong to' (Kirkpatrick 2007, p. 10). Given the available linguistic resources and emerging community norms towards different pragmatic functions of English and Chinese languages in Hong Kong, an interesting question is what governs the choice of language in interactions, and to what extent previous models of code choice are applicable. Past theoretical frameworks for language choices in multilingual settings will be discussed.

5.3   Previous Accounts of Pragmatic Aspects of Code Choice Worldwide and in Hong Kong

The use of mixed codes has always been a pragmatic phenomenon. As Muñoa (1997, pp. 528–529) identified, speakers' utilisation of more than one language choice 'is often used as a communicative strategy and … would serve as an expressive function and have pragmatic meaning', highlighting the significance of studying the pragmatic meanings of mixed codes. Existing models of code choice, including (1) Fishman's (1965, 1972, 1975) domain-based approach, (2) interactional sociolinguistic approach (Ervin-Tripp 1964; Gumperz 1964, 1982; Hymes 1967; Blom and Gumperz 1972), (3) communication accommodation theory (CAT; Bourhis 1984; Giles and Smith 1979; Giles et al. 1977, 1991), and (4) Myers-Scotton's (1988, 1998) Markedness Model, vary greatly in their pragmatic functions of code choice. By examining data from language census questionnaires, Fishman (1972, p. 441) proposes that code choices are determined by speakers' expected language norms: in Puerto Rican communities in New York City community members attach different pragmatic meanings to Spanish (solidarity) and English (status) and employ an appropriate code in a particular domain (e.g. family). Interactional sociolinguistics emphasises social constraints and speakers' goals, values, beliefs and attitudes in determining code choice. CAT scholars also acknowledge these factors but stress the importance of situational language choice, which mainly serves two pragmatic functions, namely association and disassociation. They point out that in interethnic environments speakers can choose to either dissociate themselves from out-group members and thus increase ethnic tension (through divergence or non-convergence), or associate themselves to achieve interpersonal harmony and reduce ethnic conflict (via convergence).

In the Markedness Model, linguistic varieties are pragmatically differentiated as unmarked and marked codes in accordance with a set of rights and obligations (RO) in real-life situations. Specifically, one of the varieties in a multilingual setting that is used in a number of routinized social interactions is the typical (*unmarked*) code. The non-conventional (*marked*) variety can be selected however, when a speaker attempts to change the RO set signalled by the unmarked variety. Hence in this model any change in language choices as in code-switching and code-mixing is considered as serving the pragmatic function of negotiating identity and personal relationships between participants of a speech event. The later Rational Choice Model puts more emphasis on 'intentionality in human actions' (Myers-Scotton and Bolonyai 2001, p. 12; see also Myers-Scotton 1999). There are three pragmatic filters for making a linguistic choice. Situational and social norms are the first filter. Speakers' past experiences constitute the second filter. The third, and the most important, filter is rationality: a speaker chooses a particular code based on his/her goals or attitudes and thus the language choice can optimise outcomes for the individual speaker.

Regardless of their different perspectives, these models of code choice all point to the same presupposition: speakers share certain normative systems in the society or community, and are guided by these norms in participating in social interactions and interpreting the behaviour of others in these interactions.

In the context of Hong Kong, Gibbons (1987) is the first comprehensive study of code-mixing between English and Cantonese based on his own observations recorded on a language diary. Almost a decade later Li's (1996) research on code-mixing extends the scope further to focus on the local Chinese press. In fact, the end of the twentieth century has seen the greatest surge of individual research papers in this area. For instance, Yau (1997) investigates the pragmatic aspects of language choice and code switching behaviour of the councillors and officials in the Legislative Council of Hong Kong. She states that councillors representing the grassroots are more likely to use Cantonese while those representing the professionals are more likely to use English. The different pragmatic functions of Cantonese and English are also reported in a recent study of local teachers and students: the 160 respondents to Low and Lu's (2006) questionnaires felt that using the native Cantonese language helped to bring interlocutors closer to their own culture and make them more willing to talk while English was, at times, used to avoid embarrassment in discussing sensitive topics such as sex. Luke (1998) proposes a theoretical model of 'expedient language mixing' and 'orientational language mixing'. While the former refers to pragmatic needs for mixing English words that have no stylistic equivalent in the Cantonese language for example, the latter refers to a sociolinguistic need for social solidarity.

Apart from those pragmatic meanings of different code choices, some previous analyses in the past two decades have also been devoted to exploring morpho-syntactic properties of Cantonese-English code-mixing (e.g. Gibbons 1987; Chan 1998; Luke 1998). There is general agreement that the overall morpho-syntactic structure of the mixed utterances remains basically Cantonese, with English constituents embedded into such a structure. Yet the above Hong Kong case studies are all concerned with the mixing of English terms into Cantonese and thus are not directly relevant to the present study. This is not to ignore their findings entirely however, particularly those findings about code-mixing of Cantonese and English as a common speech behaviour used by bilingual people in Hong Kong. They will be brought up for discussion where necessary. There is however one previous case study that can lend support to the findings of this research: although Chan and Kwok's (1985) book-length account is concerned with lexical borrowings and is not intended to be a code-mixing analysis, their work indeed provides some useful insights into the pragmatic motivation of English coinages that have indigenous Chinese roots. Their work focusses on Chinese words that have entered English vocabulary with special reference to the English used in Hong Kong. As will be demonstrated in the discussion (see Sect. 5.5) their analysis is helpful for explaining why certain culturally oriented Chinese words can easily find their way into English spoken and written texts in the ICE-HK.

5.4   Corpus Findings

In previous literature, empirical pragmatics has been studied through different data-gathering methods, namely, discourse completion tasks (DCTs), role plays, field notes and natural conversation (see Yuan 2001 for an overview). Unlike previous pragmatic research, I relied on data gathered from the ICE-HK corpus.[2] The most relevant mark-up for this study is the one for indigenous words (tagged as *indig*), usually followed by an English translation. There are 709 indigenous Cantonese words/ phrases[3] taken from the corpus for close scrutiny.[4] A breakdown of the local terms used across text types in ICE-HK is summarised in Tables 5.1 and 5.2. Table 5.3 illustrates the wide variety of Cantonese indigenous words used in Hong Kong English (see Appendix 1 for the full list of indigenous Cantonese expressions). The frequencies of distribution of the indigenous words across all twelve major spoken and written text types

---

[2] Unlike the British National Corpus, all ICE corpora do not provide any demographic information about the participants (e.g. age, sex, social class, first language, accent, occupation, education). No potentially concrete claims could therefore be made in this study about the ethnic identity of the speakers/writers. While one cannot be certain about their ethnicity, the speakers/writers of the texts are mainly Hong Kong residents who 'were either born in the country . . ., or moved there at an early age and received their education through the medium of English in the country concerned' according to the ICE-HK web site (see The Design of ICE Corpora @ ICE-corpora.net available online at http://ice-corpora.net/ice/design.htm, accessed 14 June 2016). It is sufficient to mention here that all informants are adults with at least a finished formal English-medium secondary-school education who are considered speakers of 'educated' English of the variety and occasionally speakers whose inclusion can be justified due to their social or public status (e.g. writers, broadcasters). Therefore, the data in the corpus material is relatively controlled for social variation.

[3] The Romanisation of the indigenous words used in the corpus is not standardised. At least two systems have been in use, that is, non-standard English spellings and the Yale transcription (cf. Matthews and Yip, 1994, p. 7). Some words (e.g. *gwai lo* / *gwailo(s)* / *gwai lou* / *gweilos* / *fan-gui-lo* 'male foreigners') take two or more orthographic forms, which have been put under the same entry in this work.

[4] There are 721 matches of indigenous words/phrases extracted from the corpus. Three local words (*haaih* 'a sigh'(1 instance), *hah* 'an exclamatory word' (2 instances), *oh* (2 instances)) were excluded from analysis because they are not truly indigenous in the sense that they also exist in British and American English and other Englishes in the inner-circle countries. I also discarded loan translations, which are in fact English: *face-reading* 'a kind of traditional Chinese fortune-telling' (1 instance); *Cantopop* 'popular music of Hong Kong' (4 instances); *stinking bean curd* 'a kind of deep-fried bean curd that stinks and is a popular snack in Hong Kong' (1 instance). There is one hit in which the <indig> tag encloses two unclear words, which are not transcribed by the corpus annotator; it is therefore ignored in this research. Excluding all these cases from the set of solutions leaves 709 indigenous expressions for analysis.

Table 5.1 Counts of indigenous words in spoken ICE-HK

ICE-HK (spoken texts)	Raw freq.
S1A: Private dialogue	**364**
Direct conversations	353
Telephone calls	11
S1B: Public dialogue	**50**
Class lessons	4
Broadcast discussions	2
Legal cross-examinations	11
Business transactions	33
S2A: Unscripted monologue	**93**
Unscripted speeches	75
Demonstrations	18
S2B: Scripted monologue	**5**
Broadcast news	2
Broadcast talks	1
Non-broadcast talks	2

Table 5.2 Counts of indigenous words in written ICE-HK

ICE-HK (written texts)	Raw freq.
W1A: non-printed non-professional writing	**67**
Student essays	67
W1B: Non-printed correspondence	**10**
Social letters	10
W2A: Printed academic writing	**42**
Humanities	42
W2B: Printed non-academic writing	**3**
Humanities	3
W2C: Printed reportage	**6**
Press news reports	6
W2D: Printed instructional writing	**11**
Administrative writing	3
Skills and hobbies	8
W2E: Printed persuasive writing	**0**
Press editorials	0
W2F: Printed creative writing	**58**
Novels and stories	58

(i.e. Tables 5.1 and 5.2 considered together) in ICE-HK are statistically significant, with the log-likelihood (LL) score of 507.40 at p-value < 0.001, taking into account of the different sizes of the text categories. When grouped into different semantic classes as in

Table 5.3 Classification of indigenous words in ICE-HK

Type of indigenous words	Freq.	%
A: colloquial formulaic sequences	226	31.9
B: Chinese/Hong Kong customs	218	30.7
C: local food and cooking	32	4.5
D: kinship terms	13	1.8
E: proper nouns (person)	43	6.1
F: proper nouns (place)	35	4.9
G: proper nouns (organisation)	22	3.1
H: Miscellaneous Cantonese vocabulary	120	16.9
Total (does not equal 100% due to rounding)	709	100.0

Table 5.4 A selection of colloquial formulaic sequences from ICE-HK

Colloquial formulaic sequences

Particles
  a₂ a Cantonese particle usually used to end an utterance
  ha a Cantonese particle for seeking agreement
  la a Cantonese particle that helps to make an utterance sound friendly and less formal
Exclamatory words with a range of emotions
  hou ging an exclamatory word for showing admiration
  aai (yo) an exclamatory word for showing regret or disgust
  sei (la) an exclamatory word for expressing worry or embarrassment
Greetings
  jou sahn good morning
  Kung Hei Fat Choy Happy Lunar New Year!
  lei ho ma how are you?
Slang
  diu you fuck; a swear word
  neih louh baan used as a vulgar slang expression in Cantonese speech; literally meaning 'you boss'
  pook gai a swear word; literally meaning 'drop dead'

Table 5.3, these indigenous words occur with different frequencies, which are also statistically significant (LL = 584.61, $p < 0.001$).

About a third (226 out of 709) of the total quantity of Cantonese code mixed in English discourse is comprised of formulaic sequences (see Table 5.4). While formulaic sequences are widespread in language use, it is difficult to define formulaic sequences due to their diversity (Lin 2013, pp. 106–107; Schmitt and Carter 2004, p. 3). The diversity has

Table 5.5 Cantonese kinship terms in ICE-HK

Kinship terms in Cantonese
ah gong maternal grandfather
ah tai gong great maternal grandfather
ah tai ma great paternal grandmother
nai nai mother-in-law
poh poh maternal grandmother

resulted in a range of terminology to refer to formulaic sequences. For instance, Wray (2002, p. 9) has found over fifty terms to describe the phenomenon of formulaic language; the common terms include *chunks, collocations, conventionalised forms, formulaic speech, formulas, holophrases, multiword units, prefabricated routines,* and *ready-made utterances.* In this chapter, as noted in the introduction, the term *formulaic sequence/language* is taken to mean a sequence, continuous or discontinuous, of words or other elements, which is, or appears to be, <u>prefabricated</u>: that is, stored and retrieved <u>whole</u> from memory at the time of use, rather than being subject to generation or analysis by the language grammar. (Wray 2002, p. 9; emphasis added)

The formulaic sequences can be long (*ho noi mo gin na* 'long time no see'), or short (*hou* 'an exclamatory word for something being good or okay'), or anything in between (*haih mai* 'right?'). They can be used to express a message or idea (*ngh yahn ji daih* 'a Chinese idiom meaning pupils are misguided by their teachers' = do not set up a wrong model), pragmatic functions (*ngoh mm duk haan* 'I'm busy' = leave me alone), social solidarity (*haih lo* 'that's right' = agreeing with an interlocutor), and to address a person (a_3 'a prefix to a name'; *baak* 'a suffix for an elderly person'). A handful of code-mixing instances (13 instances) are concerned with kinship terms as outlined in Table 5.5. I have also identified some indigenous words referring to local food (32 instances; see Table 5.6) in spoken texts and local novels and stories.

Given a rich spiritual and cultural tradition, there is no question that the Chinese have established a strong ethnic identity that can influence different aspects of the life of the average person and the code choice in which these aspects are discussed. Chinese cultural terms account for about 30 % (218 out of 709) of indigenous words in the ICE-HK corpus

Table 5.6 Some local food items in ICE-HK

Local food items in Cantonese
chau mihn fried noodles
choi sum a kind of vegetables only grown in southern parts of China
dim sum dumplings in Chinese cuisine
naaih chah tea with milk
siu yuh gap roast pigeon
tohng seui Chinese dessert

Table 5.7 A selection of Cantonese words about Chinese customs

Cantonese words about Chinese customs
bazi a person's lunar date and hour of birth
ch'i a philosophical construct in Chinese traditions; literally meaning 'a breath of air'
Ching Ming a Chinese festival for people to visit their ancestors' graves
fai chuen a piece of red paper used for decoration at Lunar New Year
feng shui shi fu an expert of the occult science
Huhng Lauh Muhng Dream of the Red Chamber
kuah a traditional Chinese wedding dress made of silk and worn by a bride
kung fu martial arts
lai see / leih sih red packets with money inside, which people exchange during lunar new year
luhng dragon
mah tung a Chinese-style toilet
tao a person's moral sense

Table 5.8 A selection of Cantonese words about Hong Kong culture

Cantonese words about Hong Kong culture
chah chaan teng a Cantonese bistro serving Chinese and western food
feng shui shi fu a person who is specialised in Feng Shui
gwai lo / gwailo(s) / gwai lou foreigners
gwaipor female foreigners
muih jai foreign domestic helpers
wet hang around with friends
yuet kuk gou tan Cantonese opera club

(see Table 5.7). Some indigenous expressions are specifically created for Hong Kong culture (see Table 5.8). The mixed Cantonese code may at times involve people's names (43 instances), names of places

Table 5.9 A selection of Cantonese proper nouns

Cantonese proper nouns (personal names, place names and corporation names)
Wong Pak an elderly man with the surname Wong
Yahn / Yan (Yan) a female name
Ngau Ngak Shan name of a mountain
Chat Gei name of a shop
Tai Ping name of a shop

(35 instances) and names of shops (22 instances), as illustrated in Table 5.9. This is a common phenomenon in Hong Kong where not every name has an English equivalent.

5.5   Discussion of Pragmatic Functions of Code-Mixing

As already outlined briefly above and illustrated in examples (2–4), a wide range of Cantonese particles and emotion-loaded words/phrases is used by Hong Kong people when they speak in English. Borrowing items from an indigenous source language is not uncommon amongst English speakers in Southeast Asia. In Singapore and Malaysia, for instance, speakers borrow the particle *la* from their respective local languages to signal interactional meanings (conveying obviousness, softening an imperative, etc.) in informal conversation, marking a high level of solidarity and familiarity among interlocutors (Kachru and Smith 2008, p. 107).

(Example 2) Yeah but uh people in Philippines is so good <indig> *la* </indig> (ICE-HK:S1A-029#51)
(Example 3) <indig> *Nah* </indig> let me tell you that is the interesting thing about Hong Kong and make that makes Hong Kong a bit of different from uhm mainland China or Taiwan (ICE-HK:S1A-013#182)
(Example 4) Yeah and <,> <indig> *wah* </indig> the song is nice (ICE-HK:S1A-029#113)

The Cantonese formulaic sequences are often used when people feel the need to express themselves explicitly, as shown in examples (5) and (6). As Gibbons (1987) points out, the direct consequence of making one's feelings or emotions explicit is that interpersonal bonding between interlocutors can be formed and solidarity strengthened. In fact, the notions of interpersonal bonding and solidarity play a prominent role in motivating code-mixing. As noted earlier, models of code choice attempt to offer a single mechanism that would account for why people use a certain language in a given situation. That single mechanism is closely related to both solidarity and interpersonal relationships. For Fishman, language choice pragmatically reflects a sociopolitical value (solidarity vs. status) between varieties and domains. For interactional sociolinguistics, CAT and the Markedness Model, the choice of language is governed by the negotiation of identity and interpersonal relationships.

(Example 5) Actually I am a member of lacrosse team also but I never go to practice because I I guess is <indig> *aai* </indig> <&> an interjection of regret </&> you know I'm lazy to uh take so long for travelling and (ICE-HK:S1A-005#231)

(Example 6) A: I think especially in Hong Kong it's a very busy city
A: And and the and the language is changing so fast
A: Even you know uh if a person who live in Hong Kong you live for one or two years and when you come back maybe you cannot catch up with the language
A: Because there are always some kind of language, newly invented, changed
Z: Yeah
Z: Changed
C: <indig> *Hou gik a* </indig> <&> Very extreme/ awesome </&>
A: Yeah (ICE-HK:S1A-009#196–203)

The pragmatic need for code-mixing to enhance relationships and solidarity is also evident in the use of Cantonese kinship terms. Hong Kong people, when speaking of their relatives, choose to address them by using Cantonese, although the English terms are by no means difficult to learn and remember. Their native language carries a sense of intimacy in the same way as they are closely tied to their relatives. Examples include:

(Example 7) It's the one thing I want in life: a happy family. My husband loves me. I get along well with my <indig> *nai nai* </indig> and relatives. (ICE-HK:W2F-001#234–236)

(Example 8) <indig> *Ah tai gong* </indig> was how my brother, sister and I called my great-grandfather. He was a very well respected old man in the village. Before dying at the age of ninety-four, he had had a rather long and extraordinary life, one that most people would like to live. He had four sons and one daughter in two marriages with my <indig> *ah tai ma* </indig> and another mistress in Kam Mun, Taiwan. None of his children stayed in the country where their father's roots lay. They went away from China to different places, and settled down in alien countries. (ICE-HK:W2F-006#2–7)

Another crucial part of ethnic identity is food. As Chan and Kwok (1985, p. 51, p. 119) point out, food is the area of Chinese culture that has the greatest impact on the English-speaking world, and the integration of Chinese-style food items can be clearly identified in speech as in examples (9) and (10), and popular writing particularly with a Chinese setting, as illustrated in example (11). Of these expressions, *dim sum, chau mihn* and *choi sum* have been discussed in Chan and Kwok's (1985) study.[5]

---

[5] The *Merriam-Webster Online Dictionary* defines *dim sum* (literally *dim* 'dot' + *sum* 'heart') as 'traditional Chinese food consisting of a variety of items (as steamed or fried dumplings, pieces of cooked chicken, and rice balls) served in small portions'. This word has its origin in the southern Chinese city of Guangdong. Another term *chau mihn* (literally *chau* 'fry' + *mihn* 'noodles') can also be found in Merriam-Webster, although with a slightly different spelling *chow mein* (see also Cummings and Wolf, 2011, p. 37). It refers to Chinese (Guangdong)-type fried noodles, which are usually served with 'a seasoned stew of shredded or diced meat, mushrooms, and vegetables'. Compared with *dim sum* and *chau mihn*, the word *choi sum* (literally *choi* 'vegetable' + *sum* 'heart') does not receive the same degree of international currency outside Hong Kong.

(Example 9) Uh we decided the end point is going be Sai Kung having <indig> *tohng seui* </indig> <&> Chinese dessert </&> (ICE-HK:S1A-100#160)

(Example 10) I mean to them may be say dogs or cats or birds I mean pigeons you know like in Hong Kong will I mean say that <?> can </?> say roast pigeon is the favourite of many people <indig> *siu yuh gap* </indig> <&> These Cantonese words refer to roast pigeon </&> okay (ICE-HK: S1B-016#114)

(Example 11) The final bang at the door signals that the living room is at last barren. The sister peeps out from her room, makes sure the clock's tic-tac would be the only lively object that welcomes her, and dashes into the kitchen. Their tongue-twisting game has exhausted much of their energy, so much so that sister is ignored. She is hungry. The family has planned to <indig> *yum-cha* </indig>, and father leaves first for the Chinese restaurant. (ICE-HK:W2F-009#64–68)

The emergence of these local food items seems to illustrate an attempt to introduce Eastern flavour, and more importantly, Chinese identity. To take this point further, an obvious cultural manifestation closely related to food is *yum cha*. The term *yum cha* (literally meaning 'drink tea') refers to a Cantonese repast in which tea drinking and *dim sum* are integral components (see examples 12 and 13). In Chan and Kwok's (1985) research, over 90 % of the 100 expatriates sampled have said they knew what this word referred to and they admitted the word was often heard in mixed gatherings of expatriates and Chinese. Thus this indigenous term has evidently played an important role in integrating foreigners into local culture.

(Example 12) Z: Yup yup sometime we go out for lunch
A: Huh uh
Z: To <indig> *yam chah* </indig> <&> having lunch in a Chinese restaurant </&> or whatever sometimes usually

I just uh get some bread and ham and make sandwiches (ICE-HK:S1A-003#959–961)

(Example 13) A: Yes but uh what we meant by family day uh nowadays is not something that we should follow

A: It's not is not so straight. But uhm maybe it is what our practice

Z: Uhm uhm uhm uhm

A: What we usually do

Z: So you would go to some <indig> *dim sum* </indig> uh place and (ICE-HK:S1A-032#235–259)

Apart from local food, other aspects of Chinese culture are also attested in the corpus data for instance, marriage (e.g. *kuah*), superstition (e.g. *feng shui*) and festivals (e.g. *Ching Ming*), which have apparently influenced the code choices used in HKE. In traditional Chinese marriage, brides have to wear a silk wedding dress named *kuah*. When moving house or choosing a burial place for a deceased next of kin or relative, a specialist of the occult science (*feng shui shi fu*) has to be consulted beforehand. Although *feng shui* (literally 'wind', 'water') might appear to be superstitious in a westerner's eye, it has been highly valued by Chinese people. *Feng shui* is a form of geomancy or a belief that the outlines and general character of definite locations would bring good luck or ill luck to the inhabitants (Chan and Kwok 1985, p. 165). A *feng shui* expert is usually hired by the rich to alter their destinies by properly situating and combining rising grounds, groups of trees, pools of water, winding roads and interior of the house for health, peace, happiness and wealth. Closely related to *feng shui*, *bazi* is a traditional technique of fortune telling that is formed from people's lunar date and hour of birth and is used as the basis for making predictions about their future. Example (14) is a perfect illustration of how the notions of *feng shui* and *bazi* operate.

(Example 14) <indig> *Wang Shi Fu* </indig> told me that the Year of the Hare would not be good for me because I was born in the Year of the Tiger. Don't do any business or investments throughout the year so as to avoid incurring losses.

> Speculation will not yield any profit for me. Especially don't invest in the property market since my <indig> *bazi* </indig> belongs to the gold out of the five elements. Investing in the stock market is only advantageous in June, September and October. Don't buy and sell stocks in the other months even though there are opportunities to reap profits because his words are always true. Don't change jobs. Stay in the original work position and the chance of promotion will come in winter. No matter how nasty my boss is, I will not quit my job. Besides, put a copper vase on my desk facing the south to increase my career luck. Remember it must be made of copper, not any other material. (ICE-HK:W2F-004#145–158)

The Lunar New Year and *Ching Ming* are two major festivals in the Chinese calendar. Basically the *Ching Ming* festival is associated with the practice of ancestral worship during which roast pigs, poultry, fruit and wine are offered to ancestors. Some vocabulary such as *lai see* and *fai chuen*, which are specific to the Chinese New Year, have entered HKE. The word *lai see* (literally meaning 'making matters propitious') refers to money given in small red envelopes to confer luck on the recipient, which is also known as 'red packet' or 'lucky money' (Chan and Kwok 1985, p. 170). The other word *fai chuen* is a piece of red-coloured paper with wishes printed on it for decoration during the Chinese New Year. Another expression for the spring festival is *Kung Hei Fat Choy*, a greeting used by both expatriates and Chinese during the Chinese New Year festival.

While *luhng* 'dragon' is widely accepted to be a symbol of the Chinese community, *kung fu* 'martial arts' is arguably another. Related to Chinese martial arts is the term *ch`i*, which literally means 'a breath of air'. One has to know how to manipulate the movement of *ch`i* across one's body when practising *kung fu*. There are some indigenous words referring to philosophy and literature in Chinese traditions. For instance, Taoism is the philosophy founded by *Lao Zi*, who proposes that *tao* (also in ICE-HK) generates everything in the world and governs people's behaviour (cf. Chan and Kwok 1985, p. 167). In the realm of literature, *Shih*

Ching 'the Book of Poems' and *Huhng Lauh Muhng* 'Dreams of the Red Chamber' refer to two influential literary works in the Chinese history.

(Example 15) A: I have no religion

    Z: Uhm but do you celebrate like for example, do you ever go to Chinese temple for any reason or, do you, do you ever do things like uhm you know on the Chinese holidays like uhm <Indig> *Ching Ming* </indig> and things like that

    Z: Do you ever, you know, uhm, you know pay respects to your ancestors

    A: Uhm uhm Uh uh, yes, I've paid respects to ancestors but I I won't go to the Chinese Temple to pray for something because I don't believe it (ICE-HK:S1A-001#331–337)

(Example 16) Good morning, <indig> Wong Pak </indig>, why not listen to the radio? Out of order again? asked the other. When you have time, <indig> Wong Pak </indig>, we can go out and practise <indig> *kung-fu* </indig> together! (ICE-HK:W2F-003#131–133)

In addition, some corpus data show a trace of indigenous terms highlighting some cultural entities specially related to Hong Kong. For example, the city has its own distinctive kind of restaurant dubbed *chah chaan teng*, which is famous for the local drink *naai chah* (literally 'milk', 'tea'). Having previously been ruled by the British, Hong Kong has created a set of expressions referring to foreign people: *gwai lo* for 'male foreigners' and *gwaipor* for 'female foreigners', and these terms have been used in locally published fiction . It is also a popular destination for foreign domestic helpers looking for jobs outside their home countries, who are usually called *muih jai* by their Hong Kong employers. Hanging out with friends is referred to by the indigenous word *wet*.

(Example 17) I think most <indig> *gwai lou* </indig> <&> Cantonese = foreigners </&> like sandwich (ICE-HK:S1A-056#825)

(Example 18) Hello, What are u doing in the Campus? Why don't go to home? I know, u go to <indig> *wet* </indig>, right? I know u always go out to look for fun. U should be more hard-working as u are a final yr. student (ICE-HK:W1B-002#167–171)

Again ethnic identity is at least partially reflected in the use of these culturally oriented indigenous words. In the above instances (Examples 17 and 18), we have seen the tendency that code-mixing of Cantonese words into English is most prevalent when the topic under discussion touches upon Chinese or Hong Kong culture. This lends support to Kramsch's (1998, p. 10) cultural model in which culture can be defined as membership in a discourse community that shares a common social space and history, and common imaginings ... We are, then, not prisoners of the cultural meanings offered to us by our language but can enrich them in our pragmatic interactions with other language users. Luke (1998, p. 156) has pointed out that objects, institutions or cultural aspects that are perceived to be inherently western are reflected in the code choice, as in the case of the mixing of English terms into Cantonese in Hong Kong. Conversely, as evidenced in ICE-HK, Cantonese words are often used for objects, institutions or cultural aspects that are perceived to be inherently Chinese. That could possibly explain why a relatively high incidence of indigenous words (218 instances/ 30.7%) has been reported in the ICE-HK corpus, mixing Cantonese into English when speakers or writers mention Chinese/Hong Kong customs. Users of HKE are able to 'put their sense of identity into words' (Prodromou 2008, p. 13) by means of code-mixing.

As well as indexing solidarity, code-mixing pragmatically serves a gap-filling function due to the absence of a semantic match between Cantonese and English words (Li 1998, p. 176; Li 2003, pp. 16–17; Luke 1998, pp. 148–149). As stated in Table 5.9, the surname *Wong* in *Wong Pak* and the mountain named *Ngau Ngak Shan* have no English translation.[6] The same applies to another name *Yan Yan*, which is a

---

[6] The word *pak* 'uncle' is usually attached to a surname to indicate an elderly person whereas the word *shan* 'hill/mountain' is usually added to the end of a name referring to a mountain.

popular Chinese given name to a female and is often adopted as an English name (simply *Yan*) for that person. Some local shops are also referred to in Cantonese rather than in English (see examples 19 and 20). All this may help to explain another major pragmatic motivation for using mixed code: the bilingual speaker may switch from one language (English) to another (Cantonese) in order to express a concept that has no exact translation (Low and Lu 2006, p. 199).

(Example 19) All Mr Wong has dealt with is the drainage pipes in relationship to the courtyard and the relation to the uh shop called <indig> *chat gei* </indig> (ICE-HK:S1B-063#92)

(Example 20) I was only twelve years old. Every Monday after school, I went to the bakery not far away from my house. <indig> *Tai Ping* </indig> was a small shop. It was quite old with little decoration, but the raisin scones and egg tarts were excellent. (ICE-HK:W2F-005#5–8)

In some cases, Hong Kong interlocutors might simply switch back to their native language for accommodation purposes—shortening social distance and easing tension—while communicating in a foreign language. The speakers might find the Cantonese terms a lot more familiar than the English equivalents. In other cases, they would inject humour as in example (21) into their English utterances with sporadic Cantonese words (cf. Low and Lu 2006, p. 199). For instance, in example (21), the mixed code, which takes the form of a full sentence (literally meaning 'you speak something'), actually implies speaker B's disbelief in what speaker Z had said: that Chinese people don't understand a story that is being told in Chinese is totally incredible. Therefore speaker B's remark is in fact a humorous mockery of speaker Z's apparently false statement. As the accommodation theory predicts, people would associate themselves to other in-group members for strengthening ethnic solidarity via convergence. They converge on their native language (Cantonese) for transmitting friendship or other desirable emotions in both speech and writing and allowing the recipients to accept communication with less stress. Similarly, Luke's (1998, p. 149) orientational language mixing model also stresses the importance of manipulating linguistic resources to realise certain pragmatic needs such as solidarity and in-group membership.

(Example 21) A: Uhm the story is that
A: Uh can I speak in Chinese version and then translate to English
A: I'm afraid that you don't
B: Uh uh uh to to save time, I think you should
A: Uh speak in
A: Okay okay
B: Yes
Z: I don't really understand Chinese uh re
A: Oh
B: Oh Uh <indig> *neih neih gong yeh* </indig> <&> Cantonese = you-should-speak </&>
A: Oh okay
A: Uhm the story is that uhm uhm the si- the si- the story teller is a <?> women </?> who is wear uh some uh sporty shirt (ICE-HK:S1A-082#27–39)

5.6   Conclusion

As noted earlier (see Sect. 5.3) there are many examples of English elements being mixed into Cantonese and this has been reported extensively in the literature. However, there is much less available information on code-mixing of indigenous Cantonese words into English. This study has therefore sought to address the issue of such an 'unconventional' code-mixing as attested in the ICE-HK corpus data with particular reference to its pragmatic motivations. Besides conveying semantic meaning, languages also carry with them pragmatic meaning. In the context of Hong Kong, the choice of English carries the speaker's goal of establishing a status of power, education and wealth whereas the use of Chinese is pragmatically associated with a symbol of ethnic solidarity. This study has shown that a wide array of indigenous expressions can be mixed with the English language, namely, colloquial formulaic sequences, Cantonese kinship terms, and local food items, some of which (e.g. *dim sum* and *chau mihn*) have attained currency in English around the world. Ethnic Chinese identity has made the mixing of Cantonese terminology into English discourse a pragmatic choice when talking about Chinese or Hong Kong customs and culture for example, *feng shui, lai see* and *gwai lo*. In the case of proper nouns, mixed code performs a pragmatic function of filling lexical gaps for Hong Kong people, when they lack knowledge of the English equivalents of some Chinese words. There are several cases of occasional code switching in full Cantonese utterances reported in this study. These rare code switching cases as well as Cantonese substitutions for some English vocabulary are simply an act of accommodation, associating speakers with other in-group members and enhancing social solidarity. It should be noted that the overarching factor of ethnic solidarity may still come into play in the cases where the absence of semantic match and accommodation is evidenced. After all, there is no clear dividing line between these pragmatic factors and they could sometimes co-exist.

While corpus data provide a useful wealth of evidence for the study of code-mixing in a way that has not traditionally been commonly used in the scholarship, they can—and should—be analysed in combination with other methodological means such as sociolinguistics interviews and ethnographic observations. The multipronged methodological approach not only adds to the complementarity of corpus linguistics with other subfields of linguistics such as pragmatics and discourse analysis where corpus-assisted studies are gaining momentum, it also serves to ascertain the motivations of the speakers and thus put the corpus findings on a much firmer footing in the context of code-mixing.

References

Ariel, Mira. 2010. *Defining Pragmatics*. New York: Cambridge University Press.
Bauer, Robert. 2006. The Stratification of English Loanwords in Cantonese. *Journal of Chinese Linguistics* 34(2): 172–191.
Blom, Jan-Peter, and John Gumperz. 1972. Social Meaning in Linguistic Structure: Code-Switching in Norway. In *Directions in Sociolinguistics: The*

Ethnography of Communication, ed. John Gumperz and Dell Hymes, 407–434. New York: Holt, Rinehart and Winston.

Bourhis, Richard. 1984. Cross-Cultural Communication in Montreal: Two Field Studies Since Bill 101. *International Journal of the Sociology of Language* 46(1984): 33–47.

Chan, Brian Hok-shing. 1998. How Does Cantonese-English Code-Mixing Work? In *Language in Hong Kong at Century's End*, ed. Martha Pennington, 191–216. Hong Kong: Hong Kong University Press.

———. 2003. *Aspects of the Syntax, the Pragmatics and the Production of Code-Switching: Cantonese and English*. New York: Peter Lang.

———. 2007. Hybrid Language and Hybrid Identity: The Case of Cantonese-English Code-Switching in Hong Kong. In *East-West Identities: Globalisation, Localisation and Hybridisation*, ed. Chan Kwok-bun, Jan Walls, and David Hayward, 189–202. Leiden and Boston: Brill Academic Press.

Chan, Mimi, and Helen Kwok. 1985. *A Study of Lexical Borrowing from Chinese into English with Special Reference to Hong Kong*. Hong Kong: Centre of Asian Studies, University of Hong Kong.

Cruse, Alan. 2004. *Meaning in Language: An Introduction Semantics and Pragmatics*. Oxford: Oxford University Press.

Crystal, David. 2003. *English as a Global Language*. Cambridge and New York: Cambridge University Press.

Cummings, Patrick, and Hans-Georg Wolf. 2011. *A Dictionary of Hong Kong English: Words from the Fragrant Harbour*. Hong Kong: Hong Kong University Press.

Denke, Annika. 2009. *Nativelike Performance: A Corpus Study of Pragmatic Markers, Repairs and Repetition in Native and Non-Native English Speech*. Saarbrücken: VdmVerlag.

Erman, Britt, Margareta Lewis, and Lars Fant. 2013. Multiword Structures in Different Materials, and with Different Goals and Methodologies. In *Yearbook of Corpus Linguistics and Pragmatics 2013: New Domains and Methodologies*, ed. Jesús Romero-Trillo, 77–103. Dordrecht: Springer.

Ervin-Tripp, Susan. 1964. An Analysis of the Interaction of Language, Topic, and Listener. *American Anthropologist* 66(Suppl. 3): 86–102.

Fishman, Joshua. 1965. Who Speaks What Language to Whom and When? *La Linguistique* 1(2): 67–88.

———. 1972. Domains and the Relationship Between Micro- and Macro-Sociolinguistics. In *Directions in Sociolinguistics: The Ethnography of*

Communication, ed. John Gumperz and Dell Hymes, 435–453. New York: Holt, Rinehart and Winston.

———. 1975. The Relationship Between Micro- and Macro-Sociolinguistics in the Study of Who Speaks What Language to Whom and When. In *Bilingualism in the Barrio*, ed. Joshua Fishman, Robert Cooper, and Roxana Ma, 2nd ed., 583–603. The Hague: Mouton.

Fu, Gail. 1975. A Hong Kong Perspective: English Language Learning and the Chinese Context. Unpublished PhD Dissertation, University of Michigan, USA.

Gibbons, John. 1983. Attitudes Towards Languages and Code-Mixing in Hong Kong. *Journal of Multilingual and Multicultural Development* 4(2–3): 129–147.

———. 1987. *Code-Mixing and Code Choice: A Hong Kong Case Study*. Clevedon and Philadelphia: Multilingual Matters.

Giles, Howard, Richard Bourhis, and Donald Taylor. 1977. Towards a Theory of Language in Ethnic Group Relations. In *Language, Ethnicity and Intergroup Relations*, ed. Howard Giles, 307–348. London: Academic Press.

Giles, Howard, Nikolas Coupland, and Justine Coupland. 1991. Accommodation Theory: Communication, Context, and Consequence. In *Contexts of Accommodation: Developments in Applied Sociolinguistics*, ed. Howard Giles, Nikolas Coupland, and Justine Coupland, 1–68. Cambridge: Cambridge University Press.

Giles, Howard, and Philip Smith. 1979. Accommodation Theory: Optimal Levels of Convergence. In *Language and Social Psychology*, ed. Howard Giles and Robert St. Clair, 45–65. Oxford: Blackwell.

Granger, Sylviane. 1998. Prefabricated Patterns in Advanced EFL Writing: Collocations and Formulae. In *Phraseology: Theory, Analysis and Applications*, ed. A.P. Cowie, 145–160. Oxford: Oxford University Press.

Gumperz, John. 1964. Linguistic and Social Interaction in Two Communities. *American Anthropologist* 66(Suppl. 3): 137–153.

———. 1982. *Discourse Strategies*. New York: Cambridge University Press.

Hymes, Dell. 1967. Models of the Interaction of Language and Social Setting. *Journal of Social Issues* 23(2): 8–28.

Kachru, Yamuna, and Larry Smith. 2008. *Cultures, Contexts, and World Englishes*. New York and London: Routledge.

Kirkpatrick, Andy. 2007. *World Englishes: Implications for International Communication and English Language Teaching*. Cambridge: Cambridge University Press.

Kramsch, Claire. 1998. *Language and Culture*. Oxford: Oxford University Press.

Levinson, Stephen. 1983. *Pragmatics*. Cambridge: Cambridge University Press.

Li, David C.S. 1996. *Issues in Bilingualism and Biculturalism: A Hong Kong Case Study*. New York: Peter Lang.

————. 1998. The Plight of the Purist. In *Language in Hong Kong at Century's End*, ed. Martha Pennington, 161–190. Hong Kong: Hong Kong University Press.

————. 2003. Code Mixing Between Hong Kong Cantonese and English. *Foreign Language Teaching and Research* 35(1): 13–19.

Lin, Yen-Liang. 2013. Discourse Functions of Recurrent Multi-Word Sequences in Online and Spoken Intercultural Communication. In *Yearbook of Corpus Linguistics and Pragmatics 2013: New Domains and Methodologies*, ed. Jesús Romero-Trillo, 105–129. Dordrecht: Springer.

Low, Winnie W.M., and Dan Lu. 2006. Persistent Use of Mixed Code: An Exploration of Its Functions in Hong Kong Schools. *The International Journal of Bilingual Education and Bilingualism* 9(2): 181–204.

Luke, Kang-Kwong. 1998. Why Two Languages Might Be Better Than One: Motivations of Language Mixing in Hong Kong. In *Language in Hong Kong at Century's End*, ed. Martha Pennington, 145–159. Hong Kong: Hong Kong University Press.

Martin, Peter. 2005. Language Shift and Code-Mixing: A Case Study from Northern Borneo. *Australian Journal of Linguistics* 25(1): 109–125.

Matthews, Stephen, and Virginia Yip. 1994. *Cantonese: A Comprehensive Grammar*. London and New York: Routledge.

Muñoa, Inma. 1997. Pragmatic Functions of Code-Switching Among Basque-Spanish Bilinguals. In *Actas del I Simposio internacional sobre bilingüismo* [Proceedings of the First International Symposium on Bilingualism], 528–541. http://webs.uvigo.es/ssl/actas1997/04/Munhoa.pdf. Accessed 14 June 2016.

Myers-Scotton, Carol. 1988. Code Switching as Indexical of Social Negotiations. In *Codeswitching: Anthropological and Sociolinguistic Perspectives*, ed. Monica Heller, 151–186. Berlin: Gruyter.

————. 1998. A Theoretical Introduction to the Markedness Model. In *Codes and Consequences: Choosing Linguistic Varieties*, ed. Carol Myers-Scotton, 18–38. New York: Oxford University Press.

————. 1999. Explaining the Role of Norms and Rationality in Codeswitching. *Journal of Pragmatics* 32(9): 1259–1271.

Myers-Scotton, Carol, and Agnes Bolonyai. 2001. Calculating Speakers: Codeswitching in a Rational Choice Model. *Language in Society* 30(1): 1–28.

Pennington, Martha, and Francis Yue. 1994. English and Chinese in Hong Kong: Pre-1997 Language Attitudes. *World Englishes* 13(1): 1–20.

Prodromou, Luke. 2008. *English as a Lingua Franca: A Corpus-Based Analysis.* London: Continuum.

Schmitt, Norbert, and Ronald Carter. 2004. Formulaic Sequences in Action. In *Formulaic Sequences: Acquisition, Processing and Use*, ed. Norbert Schmitt, 1–22. Amsterdam and Philadelphia: John Benjamins.

Wong, Cathy, Robert Bauer, and Zoe Lam. 2007. The Integration of English Loanwords in Hong Kong Cantonese. Paper presented at the 17th Annual Meeting of the Southeast Asian Linguistics Society (SEALSXVII), 31 August–2 September 2007, University of Maryland, USA.

Wray, Alison. 2002. *Formulaic Language and the Lexicon*. Cambridge: Cambridge University Press.

Yau, Frances Man-siu. 1997. Code Switching and Language Choice in the Hong Kong Legislative Council. *Journal of Multilingual and Multicultural Development* 18(1): 40–53.

Yau, Man-siu. 1993. Functions of Two Codes in Hong Kong Chinese. *World Englishes* 12(1): 25–33.

Yuan, Yi. 2001. An Inquiry into Empirical Pragmatics Data-Gathering Methods: Written DCTs, Oral DCTs, Field Notes, and Natural Conversation. *Journal of Pragmatics* 33(2): 271–292.

6

Linguistic Variation in Digital Discourse: The Case of Blogs

Abstract Wong offers a fascinating linguistic analysis of blogs in Hong Kong English (HKE), drawing on insights taken from the Corpus of Global Web-based English (GloWbE). Using an online corpus analysis interface, Wmatrix, Wong provides a reliable account of parts-of-speech categories and semantic domains that are statistically significant in the online blog postings retrieved from the Hong Kong segment of GloWbE, highlighting the linguistic variation of the HKE blog variety of digital discourse that has not been explored before.

Keywords Blogs • Digital discourse • Hong Kong English • Wmatrix • Semantic domains • Part-of-speech annotation • Linguistic variation

6.1   Introduction

Blogs (short for weblogs)[1] have become a hugely popular form of digital discourse, along with social networking sites such as Facebook and Twitter, over the past two decades or so. The rather short history of blogs can generally be marked by three phases: the mid-1990s, the late 1990s, and the beginning of the twenty-first century. In the mid-1990s, online archives of a single person's postings began to emerge, giving rise to two different types of websites: online diaries and commentary pages. Typically, these sites are regularly updated and chronologically arranged and contain postings written by an individual (or an expert in the case of commentary pages) that are made freely available to the public. It seems fairly reasonable to assume that these two forms of online language give rise to a new and important type of digital discourse that is subsequently considered to be the blog 'genre', as the key features of constant updating and inverse chronological order of online postings that can be found in these two kinds of websites can also be associated with blogs (see Herring et al. 2004). Since the late 1990s, blogs have been gaining enormous popularity, largely because of the availability of blog-publishing software and blog-hosting services, allowing potential bloggers to build personal websites and express their views much more readily than ever before. However, it is not until the turn of the twenty-first century that blogs became an important tool in politics and journalism; in the early 2000s, numerous blogs came into being and major news stories began to be disseminated through blogs.

Given the growing recognition of this newly emerging variety of digital discourse it does not come as a surprise that blogs have engendered various scholarly studies over the past ten years, such as the content analysis of blogs as raw text (e.g. Herring et al. 2004, 2005, 2007), and the rhetorical analysis of blogs as composed of multimodalities involving images, videos, audio files and hypertextual links to other blogs (e.g. Miller and Shepherd 2004). Some previous studies have also analysed the linguistic features of

---

[1] As described in Grieve et al. (2011, p. 304), the term *blog* is a shortened form of *weblog*, which was initially coined by Jorn Barger in 1977 to refer to the whole ensemble of web links he stored on this website *Robot Wisdom*.

the blog variety. For example, based on the frequency distribution of pronouns, determiners and other function words, Herring and Paolillo (2006) investigate gender differences in blogs, whereas Pushmann (2007a, b) argues for recognising the linguistic variation of blogs in corpus development. There has also been research devoted specifically to the classification of blogs into two major types, namely personal blogs and thematic blogs (see, for example, Krishnamurthy 2002). Like online personal journals, *personal blogs* are websites where an author discusses their own life. Nevertheless, blogs can also be used as a channel for bloggers to express their views on a particular theme (e.g. politics, travel, adventure, arts, entertainment and technology); these blogs are called *thematic blogs*. In addition, Herring and Paolillo (2006) divided thematic blogs into two sub-types: *filter blogs*, which contain an individual's reflections and comments on newspaper articles, often with hyperlinks provided by the writer; and *k-logs* (short for *knowledge-logs*), which provide information on a particular topic written by an expert. These common assumptions about two major blog types— personal blogs and thematic blogs—are later confirmed by Grieve et al. (2011) who identify the principal dimensions of linguistic variation across a 2-million-word corpus of blogs based on a factor analysis and then uses them to define the two basic blog registers in a cluster analysis (see also Biber and Egbert 2016).

While insightful very few of these previous accounts have analysed the linguistic properties of blogs in world Englishes. The major exception is Ooi et al. (2007) that attempts to use grammatical categories and semantic domains to analyse gender distinction and cultural identity in teenagers and undergraduates' personal blogs written in Singapore English. This is a remarkable research study as it highlights the significant difference in linguistic variation in blogs between the Outer Circle varieties of English (such as Singapore English) and the Inter Circle ones (such as British and American English) that have been the subject of most of the previous research on the genre of blogs.[2] Very little is therefore currently known about the overall linguistic characteristics of blogs written by authors of a certain regional variety of English from Outer Circle countries. The

---

[2] See Kachru (1985) for the distinction between Inner and Outer Circle.

present study is thus intended to fill this gap, and more specifically, to identify the lexicogrammatical and semantic dimensions of linguistic variation in the blog variety of digital discourse of the English language used in Hong Kong. In order to achieve this goal, a corpus of blogs and corpus-analytic techniques were utilised as discussed in the next section.

6.2   Corpus and Methodology

The data analysed here was taken from the Global Web-based English Corpus (GloWbE) made available in 2013 to all researchers at (http://corpus2.byu.edu/glowbe) (Davies and Fuchs 2015; see also Chap. 1, Sect. 1.4). Recognising the challenge to provide raw data from speakers of world Englishes, the corpus creator turned to the web, a vast and rich source of language data in electronic form, and extracted written English text from informal blogs and other web-based genres such as newspapers, magazines, company websites, and so on, yielding roughly 1.9 billion words of text from six Inner Circle and fourteen Outer Circle countries.[3] In this study, the Hong Kong subcorpus of the GloWbE corpus (GloWbE-HK) has been analysed in comparison with the subcorpus for Great Britain (GloWbE-GB) by virtue of its being the historical input variety that Hong Kong English (HKE) models on as a result of the colonial past. The GloWbE-HK subcorpus contains 12,036,809 word tokens and 144,573 word types, whereas the GloWbE-GB subcorpus is almost ten times larger in size, containing 126,954,633 words in total and 490,189 different types of words.

Both subcorpora were analysed using two corpus processing tools, AntConc and Wmatrix. AntConc (Anthony 2014) provides a whole range of useful tools—most notably, Concordance Tool, Collocates Tool, Word List, and Keyword List—for carrying out corpus linguistics research into large corpora with extraordinarily fast speed; this is especially

---

[3] The six Inner Circle countries are the USA, Canada, Great Britain, Ireland, Australia and New Zealand, while the 14 Outer Circle countries include India, Sri Lanka, Pakistan, Bangladesh, Singapore, Malaysia, Philippines, Hong Kong, South Africa, Nigeria, Ghana, Kenya, Tanzania and Jamaica.

important as the Hong Kong subcorpus of GloWbE is more than 10 million words and the GloWbE-GB is over 100 million words. In this study, keywords—or 'words that play a role in identifying important elements of the text' (Bondi 2010, p. 1), defined as those whose frequency in a corpus is statistically significant, when compared with another, reference corpus—found in GloWbE-HK were identified by comparing this subcorpus to GloWbE-GB as the reference corpus with the help of AntConc.

Wmatrix is a powerful online corpus analysis interface (Rayson et al. 2004; Rayson 2008), allowing part-of-speech tagging and semantic tagging, both of which are extremely useful for the study of linguistic variation in the genre of blogs in HKE. Indeed, one of the advantages of semantic tagging is that 'decisions on which linguistic features are important or should be studied further are made on the basis of information extracted from the data itself; in other words, it is data-driven' (Rayson 2008, p. 521, cited in Potts and Baker 2012, p. 303). As noted above, each subcorpus is a vast collection of untagged, raw component texts amounting to over 10 million words. To facilitate the calculation of keyness in the comparison of part-of-speech and semantic tags across the two subcorpora, only the first component text of each of the subcorpora[4] was loaded into its own folder in Wmatrix, where each word was annotated through the lemmatiser and part-of-speech and semantic taggers, resulting in three paired (on the basis of both words and tags) sets of frequency lists for each of the annotation methods. Once a corpus has been loaded and processed in Wmatrix, it can be treated as a point of comparison to another sample, as the corpus tool allows users to calculate key words, parts of speech, or semantic domains in a target versus a reference corpus. Key semantic domains, like key words, are assigned positive or negative log-likelihood values. Positive domains are those 'overused' in the target corpus, whereas negative domains are 'underused' in comparison to a reference corpus. To ensure a level of statistical significance, I only considered individual semantic tags with frequencies

---

[4] The first component text of GloWbE-HK contains approximately 2 million words, whereas that of the GloWbE-GB subcorpus is more than double in size, with about 5 million words.

greater than five and log-likelihood values higher than 10.83 (99.9th percentile; 0.1% level; $p < 0.001$).

6.3   Results and Discussion

Once the two subcorpora have been compared against each other, it is necessary to interpret the key grammatical categories and semantic domains to explain why particular linguistic features occur. This is accomplished by considering the relationship between the linguistic features and the style of blogs as manifested in GloWbE-HK.

6.3.1 Key Part-of-Speech Categories

Table 6.1 outlines the key part-of-speech (POS) categories that were generated by Wmatrix by comparing the first segment of GloWbE-HK with that of GloWbE-GB. The personal nature of these blog texts is immediately noticeable; these texts are both personal narratives and personal commentaries based on the key POS categories such as *to* clauses with desire/intent/decision verbs as marked by the tags *VV0* and *VVI*, and time and place adverbials as marked by the tags *NPM1*, *DA2*, *NNL1* and *ND1*. There are various verbs of cognition and desire that can be found in GloWbE-HK, which are in the top twenty examples of both the base form (*VV0*) and the infinitive form (*VVI*) of the lexical verb: these are *want, need, think, know, see, feel, like, love* and *believe* (see Table 6.2 for the frequency of these verbs). Time adverbials such as calendar months as in the POS tag *NPM1* and nominal phrases with past time reference marked by the tag *DA2* (see Table 6.3) are also used very frequently, suggesting personal narratives and reflections on life. Locative nouns as in *NNL1* including local place names, street names, districts and nations as well as nouns with direction as in *ND1* such as South Korea and Southeast Taiwan were also detected; again, these linguistic features are normally associated with a high degree of a narrative style, recounting personal adventures and travel. Such a personal, narrative style of blog writing is illustrated in examples (1)–(3). In these examples, the blogs have a clear

Table 6.1 Key part-of-speech categories in GloWbE-HK ($p < 0.001$)

Nouns	*ND1* (singular noun of direction), *NN* (common noun, neutral for number), *NN1* (singular common noun), *NN2* (plural common noun), *NNL1* (singular locative noun), *NNO* (numeral noun, neutral for number), *NNU* (unit of measurement, neutral for number), *NNU1* (singular unit of measurement), *NNU2* (plural unit of measurement), *NP* (proper noun, neutral for number), *NPM1* (singular month noun)
Verbs	*VB0* (base form *be*), *VBR* (*are*), *VV0* (base form of lexical verb), *VVI* (infinitive)
Adjectives	*JJ* (general adjectives), *JK* (catenative adjective)
Adverbs	*REX* (adverb introducing appositional constructions), *RGT* (superlative degree adverb)
Pronouns	*PNX1* (reflective indefinite pronoun *oneself*), *PPY* (2nd person personal pronoun *you*)
Determiners	*AT* (article), *DA2* (plural after-determiner)
Prepositions	*II* (general preposition), *IO* (*of* as preposition)
Others	*BCL* (before-clause marker), *FO* (formula), *FW* (foreign word), *MC* (cardinal number, neutral for number), *TO* (infinitive marker *to*), *ZZ1* (singular letter of the alphabet)

Table 6.2 Frequency of verbs of cognition and desire in GloWbE-HK

Word	POS	Frequency	Relative frequency
want	VV0	1,484	0.06
need	VV0	1,346	0.05
get	VV0	1,227	0.05
think	VV0	957	0.04
know	VV0	850	0.03
use	VV0	743	0.03
see	VV0	709	0.03
make	VV0	689	0.03
take	VV0	610	0.02
feel	VV0	508	0.02
go	VV0	487	0.02
try	VV0	451	0.02
say	VV0	450	0.02
like	VV0	442	0.02
love	VV0	437	0.02
find	VV0	421	0.02
let	VV0	373	0.02
believe	VV0	350	0.01
give	VV0	337	0.01
work	VV0	336	0.01

Table 6.3 Examples of time adverbials in GloWbE-HK

Word	POS	Frequency	Relative frequency
many	DA2	2,794	0.11
few	DA2	1,375	0.06
several	DA2	765	0.03
many_times	DA2	54	0.00
several_times	DA2	43	0.00
few_years_ago	DA2	25	0.00
few_times	DA2	24	0.00
few_months_ago	DA2	14	0.00
several_years_ago	DA2	11	0.00
few_days_ago	DA2	9	0.00
few_weeks_ago	DA2	9	0.00
many_years_ago	DA2	6	0.00
few_and_far_between	DA2	2	0.00
few_nights_ago	DA2	2	0.00
few_months_ago	DA2	1	0.00
several_days_ago	DA2	1	0.00
many_moons_ago	DA2	1	0.00
several_weeks_ago	DA2	1	0.00
few_minutes_ago	DA2	1	0.00
few_decades_ago	DA2	1	0.00

personal focus—not only in terms of the style of the blog, but also in terms of the thematic focus of the blog (e.g. physical appearance, travel and adventure).

(Example 1) However ... when I reach such age myself, it seems that although my inner self did not change much, I reach 40, I did not **want** to. I want to stay pretty and young and cute forever, which I **believe** every women would love to. <p> Nevertheless, things has not been easy since my late thirties, my skin got rougher and wrinkles grew when I laugh, as the air conditioning leads to dry air and I could not prevent it even when I put on make-up. <p> Even the make-up foundation stays in the ditches of those wrinkles (sob). I was too afraid to look at the mirror and I would face any mirrors with my back ...

(Example 2) The Rainbow Warrior came to the UK in **October** last year and I was lucky enough to volunteer for a week on board, this week turned into three months. In **April**, I came back for my second trip as a volunteer deckhand. Having had no experience at sea other than the ferry crossing to France as a kid, I had a lot to learn about life on a ship!

(Example 3) An ominous rain cloud positioned itself directly overhead and then dumped its stair rods of cold water. I've never appreciated rain so much. I was soaked through to the skin, but it cooled me down and revived me enough to continue up the steep steep slope. (I only cried a bit) <p> This was just part of section 4 to the viewing point at **Fei Ngo Shan** where we could see **Kowloon** and over to the [Hong Kong] **Island**. Even in our wet t-shirt competition state a taxi driver agreed to let us in his cab, I almost tipped him!

Interactive discourse and address foci that are commonly associated with personal commentaries can also be seen in the GloWbE-HK blog texts. The high frequency of the second person pronoun *you* (marked by the tag *PPY*, with 24,533 raw frequency of occurrence) is most obviously associated with an interactive style: *you* is a direct reference to the audience of the text. Combined with the other highly frequency key POS tag *VBR* referring to *are* (16,565 instances), the lexical string *you are* (and the contracted form *you're*) as in phrases such as *you are prepared to* and *you're about to*, the author of the blog is most likely to give advice or instruction to the reader. Examples (4) and (5) offer an insight into these personal commentaries. As expected, these blog samples are characterised by a relatively personal- and addressee-focussed tone; they are used by their authors to convey their opinions on one or more topics. The key POS tags *NN*, *NN1* and *NN2*—all referring to common nouns—give us a glimpse of the variety of topics, as illustrated in Tables 6.4, 6.5 and 6.6.

(Example 4) <p> Prepare your funds in case **you** need to buy a great domain name. **You** probably won't find the exact domain name for your company. However, if **you** are prepared to spend some money, **you** can probably get a close enough match. <p> For returning customers, consider adding special deals on the order page. Perhaps **you** would offer a choice of one half-priced product, from a selection of three or four, to say thank you for the business. This will allow **you** to move any older inventory, increase profits, while giving the customer a great deal.

(Example 5) No matter what, **you** need to look at your quitting one day at a time. The road to stopping is just a process. <p> Trying to stop smoking is an intimidating chore for even the toughest of people. Even

Table 6.4 Blog topics illustrated by the key POS tag NN

Word	POS	Frequency	Relative frequency
people	NN	5,253	0.21
media	NN	831	0.03
data	NN	689	0.03
sales	NN	398	0.02
staff	NN	387	0.02
series	NN	348	0.01
means	NN	217	0.01
fish	NN	182	0.01
fruit	NN	161	0.01
pair	NN	156	0.01
works	NN	146	0.01
$	NN	114	0.00
statistics	NN	113	0.00
Cantonese	NN	80	0.00
species	NN	59	0.00
graphics	NN	56	0.00
sperm	NN	56	0.00
duck	NN	44	0.00
folk	NN	43	0.00

Table 6.5 Blog topics illustrated by the key POS tag NN1

Word	POS	Frequency	Relative frequency
–	NN1	3,424	0.14
world	NN1	1,870	0.08
way	NN1	1,802	0.07
business	NN1	1,763	0.07
life	NN1	1,470	0.06
information	NN1	1,361	0.06
government	NN1	1,330	0.05
money	NN1	1,289	0.05
company	NN1	1,205	0.05
system	NN1	1,192	0.05
body	NN1	1,135	0.05
home	NN1	1,116	0.05
site	NN1	1,096	0.04
product	NN1	1,081	0.04
work	NN1	1,079	0.04
country	NN1	1,076	0.04
family	NN1	1,067	0.04
part	NN1	1,049	0.04
person	NN1	1,033	0.04

Table 6.6 Blog topics illustrated by the key POS tag NN2

Word	POS	Frequency	Relative frequency
things	NN2	1226	0.05
products	NN2	1033	0.04
children	NN2	975	0.04
students	NN2	955	0.04
men	NN2	760	0.03
women	NN2	742	0.03
others	NN2	696	0.03
friends	NN2	673	0.03
customers	NN2	655	0.03
windows	NN2	615	0.02
services	NN2	596	0.02
shoes	NN2	563	0.02
members	NN2	559	0.02
workers	NN2	553	0.02
users	NN2	544	0.02
games	NN2	542	0.02
results	NN2	520	0.02
parents	NN2	519	0.02
countries	NN2	519	0.02

though **you're** motivated to quit, **you** get physical and psychological rewards for smoking, and these can be difficult to give up. Use the tips **you** are about to read to decouple your emotions from your nicotine addiction and get rid of it for good.

6.3.2 Key Semantic Domains

One of the greatest virtues of the Wmatrix corpus analysis interface is that it calculates the keyness of semantic categories in texts and generates a list of positive key semantic tags (+*ve semtags*)—that is, tags that occur significantly more frequently in the target corpus (in this case, a 2-million-word subcorpus of GloWbE-HK) than in the reference corpus (in this case, a 5-million-word subcorpus of GloWbE-GB) as well as negative key semantic tags (−*ve semtags*)—that is, tags that occur significantly less frequently in the target corpus than in the reference corpus. At the time of writing, Wmatrix is the only corpus tool that affords such a facility to aid a comparative semantic analysis across two (sub)corpora. This is especially

Table 6.7 Top ten key positive semantic domains in GloWbE-HK

Item	O1	%(1)	O2	%(2)	LL
F1	13,310	0.54	11,907	0.24 + 4030.38	Food
B5	9,387	0.38	9,082	0.18 + 2398.15	Clothes and personal belongings
I2.2	13,652	0.55	17,352	0.35 + 1536.25	Business: Selling
Y2	9,870	0.40	12,329	0.25 + 1188.03	Information technology and computing
B3	6,438	0.26	7,300	0.15 + 1078.40	Medicines and medical treatment
M7	14,114	0.57	19,620	0.40 + 1065.19	Places
B1	15,287	0.62	21,872	0.44 + 991.17	Anatomy and physiology
I2.1	8,310	0.34	10,485	0.21 + 962.43	Business: Generally
O1	3,270	0.13	3,165	0.06 + 834.64	Substances and materials generally
O2	20,178	0.82	31,367	0.64 + 769.69	Objects generally

useful for the current study as it offers a complete and comprehensive account of linguistic variation in blogs that has not been carried out in the previous research, which mainly focusses on lexicogrammatical variation (e.g. Grieve et al. 2011) and (con)textual features in blog registers (e.g. Herring et al. 2005). In this section, I will then look at both the ten positive and ten negative semantic domains that are flagged as the most significant statistically based on log-likelihood (LL) scores with frequency of occurrence no less than 20 and LL cut-off at 10.83 ($p < 0.001$) in Wmatrix (see Tables 6.7 and 6.8, respectively for the top ten key positive semtags and top ten key negative semtags).

Among the top ten key positive semantic domains in a subcorpus of GloWbE-HK, the semantic category 'Food' has the highest LL score (4,030.38), containing words such as *food* (999 times), *eat* (479), *restaurant* (358), *menu* (334) and *diet* (297). In fact, considering all the texts included in GloWbE-HK, *food* is among the top 150 keywords ranked thirtieth, *restaurant* (109th) and *diet* (139th) (see Appendix 2 for a list of positive and negative keywords extracted from GloWbE-HK as a whole against GloWbE-GB as the reference corpus). Given the personal focus of blogs in HKE as described in the preceding subsection, it seems unsurprising that these blogs tend to be divided into two broad types: personal narratives of having meals at a particular restaurant as can be seen in

Table 6.8 Top 10 key negative semantic domains in GloWbE-HK

Item	O1	%1	O2	%2		LL
Z8	187,915	7.64	453,720	9.21	− 4781.62	Pronouns
K6	698	0.03	4,021	0.08	− 837.50	Children's games and toys
Z6	21,417	0.87	53,666	1.09	− 795.24	Negative
S9	4,255	0.17	13,365	0.27	− 703.85	Religion and the supernatural
A3+	68,343	2.78	153,990	3.13	− 671.33	Existing
G1.2	3,202	0.13	10,424	0.21	− 627.18	Politics
Z4	9,843	0.40	26,184	0.53	− 602.00	Discourse Bin
K5.1	5,879	0.24	16,782	0.34	− 578.08	Sports
Z5	676,170	27.48	1,394,817	28.31	− 409.69	Grammatical bin
Z1	23,444	0.95	54,699	1.11	− 392.28	Personal names

example (6); and, personal commentaries about food choices and health tips as in example (7).

(Example 6) When it was lunch time, we headed for the Po Lin Monastery Vegetarian **Restaurant**, where you could opt for regular (HK$60) or for VIP (HK$100). I first heard about this **restaurant** through this blogger, who strongly recommended the VIP option. My friends have previously tried both VIP and regular, agreeing that the VIP was … The **food** is set, which apparently hasn't changed for at least a decade! I knew that there wouldn't be any room for allergy requests, so the boy ate cheesy bacon and spinach muffins that we'd made the day before, and he was perfectly content (even refusing a spring roll!).

(Example 7) The most important step to stop as well as treat clouding towards eyesight is a really healthy **diet**. Individuals would be wise to take a **diet** program abundant with Vitamins A. With regard to hypertensive individuals, apart from ingesting Vitamin A rich **food** products, it is usually vital that you watch and maintain their own blood flow pressures to ordinary values.

The semantic field 'Clothes and personal belongings' comes second on the list of key positive semantic domains. The category comprises words such as *shoes* (564 instances), *bag* (427) and its plural form *bags* (315), *fashion* (387), *dress* (311), *jewellery* (291), and so on. If we look at the GloWbE keywords list, we can see that *shoes*, *handbags* and *jewellery* are also key, ranked at twenty-second, one-hundred and fifth and forty-first respectively. In addition, there are quite a number of keywords that refer to designer brand names such as *Abercrombie* (55th), [Louis] *Vuitton* (80th) and *Nike* (128th) and keywords that refer to specific kinds of clothing and shoes like *jerseys* (66th) and *leather* (138th).

It is worth noting that the four semantic fields 'Business: selling', 'Information technology and computing', 'Medicines and medical treatment' and 'Business: generally', taking the third, fourth, fifth and eighth places, respectively, on the positive semtags list, should be considered together as they exhibit another type of blogs, thematic blogs, that have been discussed in previous research and yet is not identifiable when only key part-of-speech categories are considered in the preceding subsection (see Tables 6.9, 6.10, 6.11 and 6.12 for words that are included in these four semantic fields). These semantic domains are often used in blog texts that are associated with high information density; while accomplishing various communicative goals, they do not attempt to tell a story, as illustrated in examples (8)–(11). Rather than providing personal

Table 6.9 Words in positive semtag 'Business: selling'

Word	Semtag	Frequency	Relatives frequency
market	I2.2	864	0.04
buy	I2.2	803	0.03
customers	I2.2	655	0.03
marketing	I2.2	585	0.02
sales	I2.2	398	0.02
store	I2.2	386	0.02
purchase	I2.2	353	0.01
shop	I2.2	306	0.01
customer	I2.2	305	0.01
trade	I2.2	304	0.01
advertising	I2.2	292	0.01
consumers	I2.2	279	0.01
sell	I2.2	260	0.01
selling	I2.2	246	0.01
markets	I2.2	242	0.01
shopping	I2.2	237	0.01
clients	I2.2	220	0.01
buying	I2.2	219	0.01
consumer	I2.2	218	0.01

Table 6.10 Words in positive semtag 'Information technology and computing'

Word	Semtag	Frequency	Relative frequency
online	Y2	1,505	0.06
internet	Y2	864	0.04
website	Y2	786	0.03
web	Y2	656	0.03
program	Y2	558	0.02
software	Y2	530	0.02
computer	Y2	509	0.02
blog	Y2	415	0.02
digital	Y2	296	0.01
websites	Y2	242	0.01
programs	Y2	237	0.01
screen	Y2	192	0.01
pc	Y2	148	0.01
it	Y2	119	0.00
laptop	Y2	116	0.00
computers	Y2	112	0.00
password	Y2	73	0.00
servers	Y2	66	0.00
analysts	Y2	58	0.00

Table 6.11 Words in positive semtag 'Medicines and medical treatment'

Word	Semtag	Frequency	Relative frequency
treatment	B3	499	0.02
doctor	B3	413	0.02
medical	B3	374	0.02
hospital	B3	342	0.01
doctors	B3	156	0.01
pills	B3	153	0.01
surgery	B3	150	0.01
medicine	B3	140	0.01
drugs	B3	134	0.01
drug	B3	133	0.01
massage	B3	131	0.01
treatments	B3	128	0.01
therapy	B3	103	0.00
tablet	B3	97	0.00
healthcare	B3	80	0.00
pill	B3	76	0.00
hospitals	B3	74	0.00
healing	B3	73	0.00
medication	B3	72	0.00

Table 6.12 Words in positive semtag 'Business: generally'

Word	Semtag	Frequency	Relative frequency
business	I2.1	1,766	0.07
company	I2.1	1,205	0.05
office	I2.1	837	0.03
companies	I2.1	501	0.02
economy	I2.1	345	0.01
enterprise	I2.1	273	0.01
businesses	I2.1	239	0.01
commercial	I2.1	216	0.01
enterprises	I2.1	210	0.01
commerce	I2.1	115	0.00
infrastructure	I2.1	102	0.00
offices	I2.1	98	0.00
firms	I2.1	96	0.00
firm	I2.1	86	0.00
agent	I2.1	86	0.00
portfolio	I2.1	81	0.00
agents	I2.1	70	0.00
co	I2.1	70	0.00
corporation	I2.1	68	0.00

comments or reflections, they present objective information on a variety of topics (e.g. marketing, software, cancer and conflicts of interest in business). Relevant keywords from GloWbE-HK include *market* (26th), *enterprises* (31st) and its singular form *enterprise* (147th), *property* (59th), *program* (60th), *prices* (121st), *management* (122nd) and *hotel* (141st).

(Example 8) Nevertheless as people get less and less **cash** to spend with **business** owners fighting harder than in the past for each **consumer**, forgetting about **marketing** can spell the conclusion for many a **company**. As opposed to cutting out his or her **marketing** effort, **businesses** really should be refocusing their **advertising** and **marketing** efforts on the people who are most likely to spend their **money** buying their **services** or **products**.

(Example 9) **Microsoft** Dynamics CRM **software** is not subject to these problems since it not only fits in ideally with employees existing work methods, **Google**, but also is also simple to plan and implement. Because it employs proven **Microsoft** platforms, **Microsoft**, training requirements are easy to understand and the **software** will be well received due to its ability to be moulded round your existing procedures. Enterprise is designed to provide higher levels of data protection using **hardware**-based encryption **technology**. It also includes tools to improve application compatibility and enables businesses to standardise by using a single **operating system** disk image.

(Example 10) The first difficulty in dealing with **cancer** is to **diagnose** the situation as accurately as possible, and this is what is **oncologist** roles start with. **Cancer** has traditionally been difficult to **diagnose**, because there are no outward **symptoms** other than pain. Even this can be delayed until the **cancer** is in a more advanced stage, leading to further complications. The use of modern equipment to **diagnose cancer** is a major breakthrough, but even in this case there has to be a suspicion that cancer may exist before the machine is used. This illustrates the importance of having routine **medical** examinations regularly, because many **cancers** can be **treated** effectively in their early stage.

(Example 11) Solving the problem of conflicts of interest in the **company** and the agent mechanism of dichotomy. One is the external mechanisms, through **capital markets**, **corporate** control **market**, Manager of **marketing**, **product** marketing, legal norms, and other external pressures, forcing the operators or major **shareholders** of the **company** to abandon those whose personal interests may, pursue **companies** maximise the benefits.

The sixth key positive semantic tag in GloWbE-HK is 'Places', which contains words such as *local* (908 hits), *area* (831), *city* (796), *countries* (519), *places* (372) and *region* (206). This is an interesting semantic field in that it is represented by specific places in the top 150 keywords list based on the total set of texts in the GloWbE-HK corpus. These places are *Hong Kong* itself (ranked 1st and 2nd) and other neighbouring regions and cities, including *China* (3rd), *Beijing* (6th), *mainland* (10th), *Shanghai* (12th), *Macau* (37th), *Taiwan* (44th), *Guangdong* (52nd), *Singapore* (74th) and *Guangzhou* (83rd). As expected, these blogs tend to focus on travel and economy but there are a few of them that are concerned particularly with cultural differences. In example (12), the blogger comments on a court case in 2013 in Hong Kong that the Court of Final Appeal had to rule on: the case concerned Ms W, a post-operative male-to-female transsexual, who fought to be recognised as a woman and for the right to marry the man she loves. The word *countries* is mentioned when a comparison in transsexual rights is made between Hong Kong and other Asian countries.

(Example 12) W We applaud W for her incredible courage to fight for her rights against our backward, closed-minded government. When **countries** all over **Asia**, including **Mainland China**, recognise transsexual rights, why does **Hong Kong** refuse to? We just hope that the Court of Final Appeal finally sees sense and allows W to enjoy a basic right all other women in **Hong Kong** enjoy—the right to marry.

The seventh most significant positive semantic domain, 'Anatomy and physiology' includes words to do with the human body such as *body* (1135 occurrences), *back* (465), *head* (395), *hair* (391) and *skin* (374). In fact, both *body* (ranked 49th) and *skin* (89th) are among the top 150 keywords when the totality of texts in GloWbE-HK is considered. Unsurprisingly these blogs are usually thematic blogs that convey information about fitness and health and beauty, as shown in examples (13) and (14).

(Example 13) This is the reality is doing a million abdominal obesity people and is shown how effectively. If you are on a daily basis to maximise your whole **body** and **muscles** beneath the **skin** for that may improve your metabolism because they are tasty and harmoniously. Without prescription make sure you know all the adverse side effects can be even more harmful like the positive state of living in this area head over to treat this problem.

(Example 14) The facial exercises primarily target the **muscles** lying underneath your **skin**. Since the exercise firm up the **muscles**, you are able to keep the **skin** smoother. This makes your **skin** more flawless and looking young. Do exercises all the time since it will keep your **skin** wrinkle-free ... By doing these exercises, you are able to enhance blood circulation. Your **skin** remains as healthy as possible and fights off any free radicals that form on the **skin**. It does not only keep your **skin** looking smoother, but it also keeps it healthy.

The last two key positive semtags among the top ten key positive semantic domains, namely 'Substances and materials generally' and 'Objects generally', appear to overlap with the other semantic fields mentioned above. For example, such words subsumed under 'Substances and materials generally' as *fat* (284 hits), *ingredients* (198) and *protein*

(61) are likely to be associated with the semantic field 'Food'; other words marked as belonging to 'Substances and materials generally' like *insulin* (159) and *glucose* (21) can also be related to the semantic field 'Medicines and medical treatment'. The same picture emerges when we consider the tag 'Objects generally'. The words that occur with this semantic tag are *things* (1,226) and its singular form *thing* (889), *product* (1,081), *products* (1,033), *model* (295) and *device* (256); when considered in context, these words are often associated with the semantic domains 'Business: generally' and 'Information technology and computing', as exemplified in examples (15) and (16).

(Example 15) The first **thing** you'll need to decide when choosing your **credit card**, is why you need one in the first place. Some people choose to get a **credit card** for **cash flow** purposes. With a **credit card**, you can make **purchases** and **buy things**, leaving your **paycheck** or other source of **income** in your bank account to draw interest. This way, your **money** will continue to grow while you continue to **buy** the **things** you need. Then at the end of the month, simply **pay** your **bill**.

(Example 16) It is no surprise, then, that **Windows** and **Android** OEMs are rather upset that **Microsoft** and **Google** are getting into the **hardware** game. 'We think that **Microsoft**'s launch of its own-brand **products** is negative for the whole **PC** industry,' says **Acer**. **Dell** and **HP** have both abandoned their plans to produce ARM-based **Windows** RT (8) **tablets**, presumably because of competition from **Microsoft**'s Surface. **Google** is at pains to point out that the **Motorola** acquisition won't impact its partnerships with **Android** OEMs, but as we've already seen with the Nexus Q—**Google's** first home-made **Android**-powered **device**—the situation is a little more complex than that.

Now let us turn to the negative semantic domains. The top key negative semtag is pronouns, which includes mainly personal pronouns such as *you* (24,533 instances), *your* (11,638), *I* (18,412), *we* (9492), *they* (8,929), *he* (7,201), *their* (6,065), *my* (5,235), *his* (4,909), *them* (3,625), *her* (2,935), *me* (2,903), *she* (2,652), *us* (2,101) and *him* (1,659). As noted above, these key semantic domains were generated by Wmatrix on the basis of a comparison between the first segment of GloWbE-HK and that of GloWbE-GB. The results of the positive key semantic domains discussed above have so far been largely compatible with those from the top 150 keywords list, which is compiled from all the texts included in GloWbE-HK using the complete GloWbE-GB as the reference corpus. However, as for personal pronouns, *you* is a positive keyword when the GloWbE-HK corpus is considered in its entirety, suggesting involvement and addressee focus. On the other hand, all the other personal pronouns are negative keywords: *I* (ranked 1st), *he* (6th), *we* (12th), *me* (27th), *his* (28th), *him* (32nd), *my* (44th), and *they* (47th). Thus, the usage of the personal pronoun *you* is the only discrepancy found between the results of key semantic domains and those of the keywords list. This finding might point to a major difference between HKE and British English in blog writing in that the bloggers in Hong Kong might prefer personal commentaries to personal narratives in the genre of online postings compared to their British counterparts and thus their blogs tend to use a personal voice and be relatively more addressee focussed to discuss and offer opinions on impersonal topics. In addition, the fact that the personal pronoun *I* is a negative keyword across the whole GloWbE-HK corpus seems to confirm this assumption as it is an important linguistic feature directly associated with a narrative style and it is underused in the Hong Kong blog postings. This probably also explains why the semantic domain 'Personal names' (the 10th key negative semtag) is under-represented in online writing as well in HKE: in personal commentaries, the author refers to and interacts directly with the audience of the text rather than someone else.

Negative key semantic domains can also give us insights into the topics that are discussed less in blogs in HKE than in those written in British English. For example, the semantic field 'Children's games and toys' including words such as *players* (288 occurrences), *player* (178), *toys* (55), *toy* (40) and *playground* (26) is clearly under-represented in online language in Hong Kong, although both *players* (ranked 13th on the negative keywords list) and its singular form *player* (36th) may in fact be related to another key negative semtag 'Sports' containing words like *game* (694 hits), *games* (544), *exercise* (392), *sports* (268), *goal* (225) and so on. Indeed the negative semantic field 'Sports' is very interesting in that many of the top 150 negative keywords are primarily concerned with football: *Arsenal* (ranked 5th), *league* (9th), *season* (16th), *team* (19th), *game* (20th), *Liverpool* (23rd), *football* (24th), *fans* (29th), *Chelsea* (31st),

Wenger (35th), *club* (37th), *Manchester* (39th), *win* (50th), *midfield* (52nd), *teams* (56th), *play* (63rd), *premier* (65th), *striker* (66th), *played* (79th), *match* (80th), *defence* (89th), *champions* (92nd), *Newcastle* (93rd), *playing* (95th), *Arsene* (100th), *Tottenham* (101st), *Suarez* (105th), *Everton* (106th), *attacking* (113th), *clubs* (118th), *manager* (122nd), *midfielder* (126th), *Persie* (130th), *goal* (132nd), *pitch* (142nd) and *Theo* [Walcott] (150th). This is clearly indicative of a predilection for discussing football in blogs in Britain rather than in Hong Kong.

Three other negative semantic domains in the top ten key negative semtags include 'Religion and the supernatural' with words such as *God* (265 instances), *soul* (170), *spirit* (158), *hell* (125), *religion* (91) and *church* (86), 'Existing' including words like *reality* (209) and *existence* (120) as well as 'Politics' containing words such as *political* (366), *democracy* (122), *vote* (118), *election* (111) and *democratic* (79). It is somewhat surprising that 'the supernatural' is not mentioned as often in GloWbE-HK as in GloWbE-GB given that the Chinese community in general is perceived to be more superstitious than the West (see Wolf and Chan 2016). But it is clearly the case that not as many people in Hong Kong as in Britain are regularly involved in religious activities such as going to church and worshipping deities. The semantic field 'politics' is also under-represented in Hong Kong's digital discourse, at least in 2013 when the GloWbE corpus was complied. It would be fair to say that people in Hong Kong, especially teenagers and young adults, are more politically conscious after the Occupy Central protests took place in 2014 and when the issue of universal suffrage is so widely discussed in preparation of the Chief Executive election in 2017.

In addition to blog topics that are under-discussed, key negative semantic domains can also be indicative of a difference in the style of blog writing between HKE and British English. The bloggers in Hong Kong appear to employ fewer negative markers such as *not* (11,680 instances), *n't* (5532), *no* (2781), *nothing* (489), *negative* (154), *nor* (152) and *none* (146) than their British counterparts, as shown in the negative semantic domain 'Negative'. Additionally, the usage of discourse markers such as *please* (425) and *right* (335) and function words such as *the* (135,086) and *and* (62,219), as in the key negative semtags 'Discourse bin' and 'Grammatical bin' respectively, appears to be much less dominant in the GloWbE-HK blog texts. This might be related to a more general stylistic difference between HKE and British English that requires further investigation of other written genres in digital discourse.

6.4   Conclusion

In conclusion, based on a corpus analysis of linguistic variation across a 2-million-word subcorpus of the Hong Kong component of the GloWbE corpus, some key linguistic features in terms of grammatical categories and semantic domains were identified, which represent significant patterns of linguistic variation for this variety of English. These blog texts tend to be personal, narrative/reflective and highly involved through the use of desire/intent/decision verbs and place and time adverbials. They are often written with a very personal tone and are concerned primarily with the blogger's own life. Given this subject matter it is not surprising that these blogs tend to be narratives. In addition, some of these blogs tend to be relatively addressee focussed—a functional pattern that seems to reflect the conversational style of these blogs and their author's desire to express their views and have their blogs read, enjoyed and commented on by their readers, and perhaps in particular by their friends. The high frequency of the second person pronoun *you* clearly indicates that these online postings are written in the form of personal commentaries, referring directly to, and interacting with, the readership. More often than not, these commentary blogs use a personal voice to discuss and offer opinions on impersonal topics. Given the nature of the medium—a personal website that is read and commented on by others—the fact that this personal tone is generally adopted is not surprising. Apart from personal blogs, another basic type of blogs—thematic blogs—that are discussed in previous research can also be found in the GloWbE-HK corpus, when semantic domains are considered. It has been demonstrated that blogs that are concerned with such topics as business, information technology and medical treatment are written in a rather formal style and are used by their authors to convey information on a particular impersonal topic. These blogs read like newspaper and academic articles because of their similar communicative goals. The major division in blog writing is therefore based on topic: blogs that focus on their author's lives are distinguished from blogs that focus on thematic topics. The basic division between personal blogs and thematic blogs, posited in the introduction and past research for Inner Circle varieties of English (e.g. British and American English), therefore, seems to hold true for HKE.

References

Anthony, Laurence. 2014. *AntConc* (Version 3.4.3) [Computer Software]. Tokyo, Japan: Waseda University. http://www.laurenceanthony.net/soft ware.html. Accessed 14 June 2016.

Biber, Douglas, and Jesse Egbert. 2016. Register Variation on the Searchable Web: A Multi-Dimensional Analysis. *Journal of English Linguistics* 44(2): 95–137.

Bondi, Marina. 2010. Perspectives on Keywords and Keyness: An Introduction. In *Keyness in Texts*, ed. Marina Bondi and Mike Scott, 1–18. Amsterdam and Philadelphia: John Benjamins.

Davies, Mark, and Robert Fuchs. 2015. Expanding Horizons in the Study of World Englishes with the 1.9 Billion Word Global Web-Based English Corpus (GloWbE). *English World-Wide* 36(1): 1–28.

Grieve, Jack, Douglas Biber, Eric Friginal, and Tatianna Nekrasova. 2011. Variation Among Blogs: A Multi-Dimensional Analysis. In *Genres on the Web: Corpus Studies and Computational Models*, ed. Alexander Mehler, Serge Sharoff, and Marina Santini, 303–322. New York: Springer-Verlag.

Herring, Susan, and John Paolillo. 2006. Gender and Genre Variation in Weblogs. *Journal of Sociolinguistics* 10(4): 439–459.

Herring, Susan, Lois Ann Scheidt, Inna Kouper, and Elijah Wright. 2007. A Longitudinal Content Analysis of Weblogs: 2003–2004. In *Blogging, Citizenship and the Future of Media*, ed. Mark Tremayne, 3–20. London: Routledge.

Herring, Susan, Lois Ann Scheidt, Elijah Wright, and Sabrina Bonus. 2004. Bridging the Gap: A Genre Analysis of Weblogs. In *Proceedings of the 37th Hawaii International Conference on System Sciences*, 101–111. Los Alamitos, CA: IEEE Computer Society Press.

———. 2005. Weblogs as a Bridging Genre. *Information, Technology and People* 18(2): 142–171.

Kachru, Braj. 1985. Standards, Codification and Sociolinguistic Realism: The English Language in the Outer Circle. In *English in the World: Teaching and*

Learning the Language and Literatures, ed. Randolph Quirk and Henry Widdowson, 11–36. Cambridge: Cambridge University Press.

Krishnamurthy, Sandeep. 2002. The Multidimensionality of Blog Conversations: The Virtual Enactment of September 11. Paper presented at Internet Research 3.0, Maastricht, The Netherlands.

Miller, Carolyn, and Dawn Shepherd. 2004. Blogging as Social Action: A Genre Analysis of the Weblog. *The University of Minnesota Digital Conservancy.* http://conservancy.umn.edu/handle/11299/172818. Accessed 14 June 2016.

Ooi, Vincent B.Y., Peter K.W. Tan, and Andy K.L. Chiang. 2007. Analysing Personal Weblogs in Singapore English: The WMatrix Approach. In *eVarIEng* (Journal of the Research Unit for Variation, Contacts, and Change in English), Vol. 2: *Towards Multimedia in Corpus Studies.* Finland: University of Helsinki. http://www.helsinki.fi/varieng/series/volumes/02/ooi_et_al/. Accessed 14 June 2016.

Potts, Amanda, and Paul Baker. 2012. Does Semantic Tagging Identify Cultural Change in British and American English? *International Journal of Corpus Linguistics* 17(3): 295–324.

Pushmann, Cornelius. 2007a. Blogs or Flogs? Genre Conventions and Linguistic Practices in Corporate Web Logs. Invited Talk presented at the Telematica Instituut, Enschede, The Netherlands. http://www.slideshare.net/coffee001/blogs-or-flogs-genre-conventions-and-linguistic-practices-in-corporate-web-logs/. Accessed 14 June 2016.

———. 2007b. Corpora, Blogs and Linguistic Variation—Arguments for Using Structured Web Data in Corpus Development. Invited Talk presented at the University of Paderborn, Germany. http://www.slideshare.net/coffee001/corpora-blogs-and-linguistic-variation-paderborn. Accessed 14 June 2016.

Rayson, Paul. 2008. From Key Words to Key Semantic Domains. *International Journal of Corpus Linguistics* 13(4): 519–549.

Rayson, Paul, Dawn Archer, Scott Piao, and Tony McEnery. 2004. The UCREL Semantic Analysis System. In *Proceedings of the Workshop on Beyond Named Entity Recognition Semantic Labelling for NLP Tasks in Association with 4th International Conference on Language Resources and Evaluation (LREC 2004),* 25th May 2004, Lisbon, Portugal, pp. 7–12.

Wolf, Hans-Georg, and Thomas Chan. 2016. Understanding Asia by Means of Cognitive Sociolinguistics and Cultural Linguistics—The Example of GHOSTS in Hong Kong English. In *Communicating with Asia: The Future of English as a Global Language*, ed. Gerhard Leitner, Azirah Hashim, and Hans-Georg Wolf, 249–266. Cambridge: Cambridge University Press.

7

Conclusion

Abstract While the advantages of using corpora in linguistic research
have been widely recognised, researching into world Englishes through
the exploitation of corpus techniques has been a relatively new endeavour.
Having said that, the creation of the International Corpus of English
(ICE) is undoubtedly key to the emerging corpus-based approach in the
field. 'Hong Kong English: Exploring lexicogrammar and discourse from
a corpus-linguistic perspective' has benefited significantly from the ICE
Hong Kong corpus and the Global Web-based English (GloWbE) corpus
for obtaining fairly large representative samples of Hong Kong English
(HKE). In this chapter, Wong provides brief summaries of case studies
concerning different structural/discoursal features of this new English
variety and discusses some emergent issues arising from her study,
reaffirming the status of HKE as an emerging nativised variety of English.

Keywords Corpus-based research into World Englishes • Structural/
discoursal features • Emergent issues • Nativisied status of Hong Kong
English

© The Author(s) 2017   **155**
M. Wong, *Hong Kong English*,
DOI 10.1057/978-1-137-51964-1_7

7.1   Summary of Major Corpus Findings

While the advantages of using corpus data in linguistic research have been widely recognised, researching into world Englishes through the exploitation of corpus-linguistic tools has been a relatively new endeavour. Having said that, the creation of the International Corpus of English (ICE) is undoubtedly the key to the emerging corpus-based approach. Since its inception in the late 1980s, the ICE project has successfully compiled comparable English corpora for a number of English-speaking countries: Great Britain, East Africa, India, New Zealand, Philippines and Singapore. Specifically, the Hong Kong component of ICE (ICE-HK) was completed and available for public use in 2006. The current study has benefited significantly from the ICE-HK corpus that provides a fairly large representative sample of Hong Kong English (HKE) without which any empirical analyses of HKE would have been impossible. In the following, a summary of the major corpus findings that have been explored in this book will be provided.

Chapter 2 reports on a quantitative and qualitative account of the use of tag questions in HKE. About 200 instances of question tags were extracted from the corpus. Tag questions are more than nine times as frequent in spoken texts as in written texts. Hong Kong speakers of English tend to disproportionately use more positive–positive tag constructions (e.g. *It's pretty, is it?*) than native English speakers, yielding a high rate of new varietal tag question production. *Is it?* is used as a universal question tag. Results concerning pragmatic functions reveal a higher use of 'confirmatory' tags encouraging participation of speakers in conversation. These tendencies of tag questions in HKE can be explained by influence from the substrate language Cantonese in that the Cantonese tag *hai6-m4hai6* is used invariantly for confirmation in conversation.

Chapter 3 considers collective nouns, with particular reference to subject-verb agreement/concord patterns. It examines singular collective nouns as subjects and how the following verb or pronoun agrees with them in number as well as assessing previous claims that concord variations with collective nouns are semantically or pragmatically motivated by the traditional 'collectivity vs individuality' principle and the semantics of the following verb phrase. It has been found that singular concord is the preferred choice in over 80 % of instances. It has also demonstrated that convention rather than semantic/pragmatic motivation plays a crucial role in concord patterns with collective nouns, with individual collective nouns showing their own preferences for a singular or plural form. Compared with tag questions, the substrate influence is far less noticeable in the case of collective nouns, as Cantonese only has collective classifiers rather than collective nouns and does not have any subject-verb agreement as in English.

Given that expressions of gratitude often occur as functional lexical chunks such as *thanks* and *thank you*, Chap. 4 focusses in particular on the use of such units and longer formulaic sequences of gratitude such as *thanks a lot* and *thank you very much* in data from the ICE-HK corpus. The results show that HKE speakers do not employ the wide variety of thanking strategies investigated in previous literature. Their expressions of gratitude are usually brief, with *thanks* and *thank you* being the most common forms of gratitude expression. They are frequently used as a closing signal and as a complete turn. Repetitive gratitude formulae and appreciation of the interlocutors in a single turn as well as across turns are exceedingly rare, suggesting that Chinese people are being too reserved to express their gratitude openly and explicitly. Responses to an act of thanking seem to be infrequent in ICE-HK and only a few strategies are represented. The chapter also demonstrates the close connection between substrate influence and the preference for brief and limited expressions of gratitude in HKE, suggesting that there is a general tendency to play down compliments in Cantonese.

Chapter 5 provides a qualitative and partly quantitative account of the code-mixing phenomenon in HKE. There have been many extensive studies of English elements being mixed into Cantonese in the literature but there is much less information available on code-mixing of indigenous Cantonese words into English. My central argument is that this kind of unexplored code-mixing pattern could be related to ethnic solidarity and identity. Some 700 instances of mixed code taken from the ICE-HK corpus were then examined. A high incidence of Cantonese colloquial formulaic sequences and cultural expressions in the spoken and written texts of the corpus suggests that code-mixing is a potential solidarity marker signalling in-group membership. Other motivations for code-mixing such as the absence of a semantic match between Cantonese proper nouns and their English translations have also been discussed.

Based on a 2-million-word sample of the Hong Kong subcorpus of the Corpus of Global Web-based English (GloWbE-HK) Chap. 6 attempts to reveal the linguistic variation of the blog variety of digital discourse in HKE using the online corpus analysis interface Wmatrix. A close analysis of part-of-speech and semantic annotations reveals that these blog texts tend to be personal narratives and personal commentaries. The key part-of-speech categories clearly indicate a highly personal, narrative style in these texts, which tend to focus on discussion of personal life, as manifested in the use of different verbs of cognition and desire. The second person pronoun *you* is typically associated with personal commentaries with its interactive style and addressee focus. As revealed by the key semantic domains, while personal blogs are common in GloWbE-HK, some of the blogs can actually be classed as thematic blogs in that these blogs are written in a rather formal style, presenting objective information on a variety of impersonal topics such as business, information technology, and medicines and medical treatment. It was therefore concluded that there are two basic types of blogs: personal blogs and thematic blogs in HKEas in the Inner Circle varieties of English such as British English and American English on which the traditional classification of blog registers is based.

7.2 Emergent Issues

There are two discourse particles—*okay* and *actually*— that are used very frequently by HKE speakers, although they have not been included in the present discussion due to space limitations. Let us begin by looking at *okay*. In everyday conversation, speakers use *okay* with a rising intonation to request confirmation and hearers use the same particle to respond, signalling comprehension (Aijmer, 2002, p. 52). In the ICE-HK data, it is clear that some tokens of *okay* are not used for soliciting and giving confirmation in a two/multiparty interaction. Rather, it occurs very commonly in extended turns by a single speaker, where it functions as a meaningless filler.[1] There is an element of register variation here: this discourse marker is more likely to be used in demonstrations (S2A) and class lessons (S1B) where one speaker normally dominates the talk and is allowed to take an extended turn for delivering information and instructions, as illustrated in the following examples from these two registers.

(1) (Example 1) <ICE-HK:S1B-017#144:1:A> While he was committing a crime he was arrested **okay** then we will say that the policeman caught the criminal red handed **okay**

(2) (Example 2) <ICE-HK:S1B-010#95:1:A> **Okay** so all these are are very clearly reveal to us **okay** uh in the first act and that's why when you look at the first act the most important thing is this establishment of Zhou Pu Yuan's position as the authority in the family and everyone in the family has to submit to his or to his rule **okay**

(3) (Example 3) <ICE-HK:S2A-056#123:1:A> And uhm when you graduate by the time you graduate okay you might be interested to know that in fact for selected resources they are also open to Hong Kong U Alumni **okay**

(4) (Example 4) <ICE-HK:S2A-058#68:1:A> Whatever product Nuskin is marketing **okay** there is one mortal guideline or principle behind it

The use of *okay* as a gap filler has been documented in the Nigerian variety of English in that '[i]t functions to provide the speakers the opportunity to better organise their thoughts' (Adegbija and Bello, 2001, p. 92), along with other senses of *okay*, which are peculiar to Nigerian English.[2]

Now we turn to *actually*. The most common use of *actually* is as a discourse modifier, functioning as a pragmatic softener with face-saving effect and as a marker of topic shift (Aijmer, 1986; Cheng and Warren, 2000; Oh, 2000; Taglicht, 2001). However, there is an emerging use of *actually* as 'a signal of contemplation' as in Xhosa English (de Klerk,

---

[1] *Okay* has also acquired a new sense in code-mixing contexts, meaning 'quite', for example, *go3 neoi5zai2 okay leng3*; that girl quite good-looking; 'That girl looks pretty good'.

[2] For example, an interesting sense of *okay* in Nigerian English is to convey a rebuke, calling for something unpleasant to stop (Adegbija and Bello, 2001, p. 93). This is not the case in HKE.

2005, p. 282). De Klerk (2005, p. 282) offers a good description of this usage of *actually*.

> While not mentioned in current writing on the topic, another function of *actually* emerged from the data which is closely linked to one of the primary functions of the discourse marker *well*, namely to serve as a 'quasi-linguistic "mental state" interjection', bringing with it the suggestion of continuation, prospecting something to follow. In this sense, some uses of *actually* are 'evincive' (Schourup, 1985), indicating that the speaker is mentally cogitating or consulting with him- or herself before proceeding.

Several uses of *actually* in the ICE-HK corpus illustrate this contemplative function: in both examples (5) and (6), *uh* and *uhm* emphasise the act of cogitation taking place while talking.

(5) (Example 5) <ICE-HK:S1A-046#1:1:A> *Uh* **actually** *uhm*, it is *uhm*, an English Project, maybe I would like you know first

(6) (Example 6) <ICE-HK:S1A-014#X30:1:Z> She said I make it lighter and and I said no no no
<ICE-HK:S1A-014#X31:1:Z> It's [The speaker's hair is] light enough already
<ICE-HK:S1A-014#32–5:1:A> Yeah
<ICE-HK:S1A-014#33:1:A> *Uh hah*
<ICE-HK:S1A-014#34:1:A> *Uhm uhm*
<ICE-HK:S1A-014#35:1:A> **Actually** you like him to cut your hair
<ICE-HK:S1A-014#X36:1:Z> He did it so good

Further evidence of the existence of this usage comes from the collocation of *actually* with *you know, I was like, sort of, well, maybe, I mean* and *I think*, all of which suggest a lack of uncertainty. The examples (10) and (11) even show the use of *actually* with a series of these collocates in just a single turn by the same speaker.

(7) (Example 7) <ICE-HK:S1B-047#157:1:A> Well let me tell you
<ICE-HK:S1B-047#158:1:A> I think the government need to work out their own better cooperation and planning

<ICE-HK:S1B-047#159:1:A> Because here's the Marine Department who say hey this is from land refuge
<ICE-HK:S1B-047#160:1:A> *You know* **actually** you beach goers you know you hikers you barbecue

(8) (Example 8) <ICE-HK:S1A-098#138:1:A> No I'm I'm not *I'm that time is like* that last time *I was like* **actually** asking for your advice not not giving advice to you

(9) (Example 9) <ICE-HK:S1A-047#164:1:A> Red badges were people like Elizabeth and Norman *you know* people **actually** *sort of* getting their *you know sort of* getting their hands dirty doing things

(10) (Example 10) <ICE-HK:S1A-100#253:1:B> And okay my hair is kind of in a way but it's always been like that and I wash my hair everyday anyway
<ICE-HK:S1A-100#254:1:B> I don't know why **actually** I I caught that *uhm, well* it's not something you catch *maybe I don't know* but *uhm* I had that one I was in Guangzhou

(11) (Example 11) <ICE-HK:S1B-079#X322:1:Z> *Uhm right* let let's let's delete the *uh* **actually** *I mean it's supposed uh I think* let's throw that **actually**

7.3 Final Remarks: HKE as an Emerging Nativised Variety of English

It would be useful in this final section to revisit the notion of nativisation first raised in the introduction and why it is particularly important for HKE to establish its status as an emerging nativised variety of English in the context of the evolution of postcolonial Englishes. In Schneider's (2003, 2007) dynamic model of the evolution of new Englishes, nativisation represents the third phase in a sequence of five stages that is posited to be characteristic of the emergence of non-native varieties of English worldwide.

> As the English language has been uprooted and relocated throughout colonial and postcolonial history, New Englishes have emerged by undergoing a functionally uniform process which can be described as a progression of five

characteristic   stages: FOUNDATION,   EXONORMATIVE
STABILISATION,   NATIVISATION,   ENDONORMATIVE
STABILISATION, DIFFERENTIATION. (Schneider, 2003, p. 243)

At the risk of some oversimplification, the five phases can be summarised as follows.

Phase 1—Foundation: The English language is transported to a new (colonial) territory.

Phase 2—Exonormative stabilisation: A growing number of English settlers/speakers reside in the territory, whose language is the input variety and is considered as a role model of language standards and norms.

Phase 3—Nativisation: As the indigenous population of competent bilingual L2 speakers steadily rise, the English language becomes an integral part of the local linguistic repertoire and undergoes a characteristic restructuring process termed 'structural nativisation'.

Phase 4—Endonormative stabilisation: A new variety of English emerges with generally accepted local standards and norms. English is used as a/an (co-)official language and a medium of communication in administration, education, academia and the press.

Phase 5—Differentiation: The new English variety is gradually develops a wide range of regional and social dialects.

Essentially, the progression from one stage to the next in the evolutionary cycle is primarily based on two inter-related factors: group interaction and identity construction. Both factors are motivated by the interaction between the indigenous people (the IND strand) and the new settler community (the STL strand). The growing social and communicative interaction between the two strands gives rise to a new hybrid identity, which, at the linguistic level, manifests itself in a new variety of English. As demonstrated in this book, the interaction between the IND and the STL strands is particularly evident in the way indigenous lexical terms and grammatical constructions are incorporated in the linguistic repertoire of the local community. A recent survey has indicated that a new type of basilect HKE has been generally accepted by at least the subscribers of a Hong Kong-based Facebook page, *Kongish Daily*, based on semi-structured interviews conducted by the founders of the site (Wong et al., 2016). As local norms have emerged and are now increasingly accepted as part of a localised variety of English, present-day HKE can be viewed as being a newly emerging, nativised variety of English.

References

Adegbija, Efurosibina, and Janet Bello. 2001. The Semantics of 'Okay' (OK) in Nigerian English. *World Englishes* 20(1): 89–98.

Aijmer, Karin. 1986. Why Is *Actually* So Popular in Spoken English? In *English in Speech and Writing: A Symposium*, ed. Gunnel Tottie and Ingegerd Bäcklund, 119–129. Stockholm: Almquist and Wiksell.

———. 2002. *English Discourse Particles: Evidence from a Corpus*. Amsterdam and Philadelphia: John Benjamins.

Cheng, Winnie, and Martin Warren. 2000. The Hong Kong Corpus of Spoken English: Language Learning Through Language Description. In *Rethinking Language Pedagogy from a Corpus Perspective*, ed. Lou Burnard and Tony McEnery, 81–104. Frankfurt: Peter Lang.

De Klerk, Vivian. 2005. The Use of *Actually* in Spoken Xhosa English: A Corpus Study. *World Englishes* 24(3): 275–288.

Oh, Sun-Young. 2000. *Actually* and *In Fact* in American English: A Data-Based Analysis. *English Language and Linguistics* 4(2): 243–268.

Schneider, Edgar. 2003. The Dynamics of New Englishes: From Identity Construction to Dialect Birth. *Language* 79(2): 233–281.

———. 2007. *Postcolonial English: Varieties Around the World*. Cambridge: Cambridge University Press.

Taglicht, Joseph. 2001. Actually, There's More to It Than Meets the Eye. *English Language and Linguistics* 5(1): 1–16.

Wong, Nick, Alfred Tsang, and Pedro Lok. 2016. The Emergence of an Overnight Success of the 'Kongish' Identity: How the Basilect Hong Kong English Becomes Prominently Preferred as a Discernible Trend on Facebook. Paper presented at *Sociolinguistics Symposium 21*, 15–18 June 2016, Universidad de Murcia, Spain.

Appendix 1: Indigenous Cantonese Expressions in ICE-HK (Divided into Different Categories and Arranged Alphabetically)

Colloquial Formulaic Sequences (226 Instances)

a₁ an interjection to show surprise, similar to English word *oh*
    a₂ a Cantonese particle usually used to end an utterance
    a₃ a prefix to a name
    ai / ay a Cantonese particle for showing exclamation
    aiya / aieeyah a Cantonese particle for showing exclamation
    baak a suffix for an elderly man for example, 'His nickname is Leung baak'
    cheng sui-sam che mun please mind the train door
    cheuih yi I don't mind
    daaih a prefix for being elder or big
    dai yaht jaaam hai Jung Wan the next station is Central
    dend send a message via email, phone, etc.; literally meaning 'throw'
    dim so now what? Or how
    dim duhk / dim gong how to say it in English
    diu you fuck; a swear word
    dor tsai thank you
    fight wa nonsense

© The Author(s) 2017
M. Wong, *Hong Kong English*,
DOI 10.1057/978-1-137-51964-1

gam yeuhng just like this
gei hou a not bad
gel fail in one's study (Note: this usage occurs only once in an informal letter presumably written by a university student talking about his study (W1B-011#84); it represents a rather unusual, idiosyncratic language form and the more common form should be *chaau*.)
gihng super
go douh there
ha a Cantonese particle for seeking agreement
hai mee-yeh see what's the matter?
haih (la) yes
haih lo that's right
haih mai right?
haih me is that right?
haih meih wah what did you say?
haih uhm haih uh is it?
hei (hei) a Cantonese particle used to draw attention from other speakers, sometimes showing annoyance
ho an exclamatory word
ho noi mo gin na long time no see
hou (hou) gik a an exclamatory word for something being extremely good or awesome
hou an exclamatory word for something being good or okay
hou ging an exclamatory word for showing admiration
hou mei douh a it's delicious
hou yeah an exclamatory word for showing approval
ji a Cantonese measure word that describes the shape of an object as a stick
ji-seen an exclamatory word for showing annoyance
jou sahn / *jou sun* good morning
jun hai truly
Kung Hei Fat Choy Happy Lunar New Year!
la a Cantonese particle that helps to make an utterance sound friendly and less formal
lang good-looking
lei ho ma how are you?

leuih chih dan gou gei yeh something similar to cake
lo an emphatic particle in Cantonese
m`goi (m`goi) thanks
m`oi m`oi no, thanks
mee-yeh wa what did you say?
mihng baahk I understood
mou a I haven't got it
mou liu inane; this Cantonese word is typically used in the context in which someone is doing something foolish or doing something without a clear purpose in mind.
mutyeh what?
nah this Cantonese word is used to draw attention from other speakers
ne go ngh ji mei I don't have a clue
neih douh here
neih haih louh baan you're the boss
neih louh baan used as a vulgar slang expression in Cantonese speech; literally meaning 'you boss'
neih neih gong yeh used as a vulgar slang expression showing disbelief in Cantonese speech; literally meaning 'you speak something'
aai (yo) an exclamatory word for showing regret or disgust
aai a / aai yah an exclamatory word for showing surprise
ngh gei dak I've forgotten what I said
ngh goi please
ngh haih (ngh haih) no
ngh sik don't know
ngh sik gong don't know what to say
ngh yahn ji daih a Chinese idiom meaning pupils are misguided by their teachers
ngoh an exclamatory word for showing agreement
ngoh douh haih aam aam sik ga I just know about it (not long before)
ngoh gok dak I think
ngoh mm duk haan I'm busy
pook gai a swear word; literally meaning 'drop dead'
sei (la) an exclamatory word for expressing worry or embarrassment
sihk daan gou eat cake
wa(h) an exclamatory word for showing admiration

wai used to draw attention from other speakers

wong bak dan a rude expression meaning a stupid and bad person

yung-yung-yung an onomatopoeic word for the sound produced by a bee

Chinese/Hong Kong Customs (218 Instances)

ang one of the structural units of a traditional Chinese building

bazi a person's lunar date and hour of birth

ch`a shou a building block of traditional Chinese architecture

ch`an meditation in Buddhist tradition

ch`i a philosophical construct in Chinese traditions; literally meaning 'a breath of air'

ch`ung-kung a double tier in traditional Chinese architecture

chah chaan teng a Cantonese bistro serving Chinese and western food

chi hsin a type of arrangement of building blocks of traditional Chinese architecture

Ching Ming a Chinese festival for people to visit their ancestors' graves

chuen fong one of three main elements of pillars in traditional Chinese buildings, along with *dao fong* and *hin chi*

compradore a Chinese agent of a British corporation

dak ji tai kwahn meih traditional Chinese virtues

dao fong one of three main elements of pillars in traditional Chinese buildings, along with *chuen fong* and *hin chi*

fai chuen a piece of red paper used for decoration at Lunar New Year

fend ya hsiung three main sections of the Book of Poems; literally meaning *wind, grace* and *ode* respectively

feng shui shi fu a person who is specialised in Feng Shui

feng-ch`i satire

gang lihn security guards

gihng gwo to pass an examination with flying colours; literally 'super pass'

gihng gwo faahn a dinner for wishing everybody best of luck with their exams *gihng gwo leih sih* a red packet for wishing the recipient best of luck with his/her exams

Gong Saan Yuh Chih Do Fun a TV quiz show in Hong Kong

gwai lo / gwailo(s) / gwai lou / gweilos / fan-gui-lo adult male foreigners

gwaipor adult female foreigners

hau kung two tiers of jutting in traditional Chinese architecture

hin chi one of three main elements of pillars in traditional Chinese buildings, along with *chuen fong* and *dao fong*

hua kung major bearing blocks at the rear of a traditional Chinese building

Huhng Lauh Muhng Dream of the Red Chamber

hung piu a kind of lottery in traditional Chinese society

jen humaneness

jen-hsing the human nature

kaifong neighbours

kuah a traditional Chinese wedding dress made of silk and worn by a bride

kung arms, part of *tou kung* of a traditional Chinese building

kung fu martial arts

lai see / leih sih red packets with money inside, which people exchange during the Lunar New Year

lau sung (wah) the language of the older brothers; slang for Mandarin

lauh guhk uaahn fuh yuh hau gung bouh testimonies of destitutes staying in Po Leung Kuk (a charitable organisation)

lu tou major bearing blocks at the front of a traditional Chinese building

luhng dragon

mah tung a Chinese-style toilet

man sze chit literature, history and philosophy in classical Chinese

mihng dak gaak maht sapientia et virtus; the motto in classical Chinese of the University of Hong Kong

muih jai (foreign) domestic helpers

ngam chaai an undercover detective

p`ai lou one of the main components of Sheng Mu Miao, a traditional Chinese building

peih neuih domestic servant

pipa a Chinese musical instrument with several strings on a long piece of wood that is played by pulling or hitting the strings with the fingers

po piu a kind of lottery in traditional Chinese society

sau jai fasting or abstaining from food for a certain period on some religious occasions

sei ngaahn jai a bespectacled man

seuhng tohng a ritual practised in traditional Chinese marriage

Shih Ching the Book of Poems; the first-ever comprehensive collection of approximately 300 classical Chinese literary works written in the period from the eleventh century to the sixth-century BCE

t`ai-chi-ch`iian a kind of physical exercise that involves slow movement and is used for meditation

t`iao / tiao an extension of traditional Chinese architecture

t`ien-jen-ho-i the idea of unity of heaven and humanity

t`ien-tao the way of heaven

t`o chiao a building block of traditional Chinese architecture

tai-tai literally 'see see'; in the corpus, it specifically refers to a kind of service offered by some local pet shops that look after animals for a short period of time when the owners go on a trip

tan kung a type of arrangement of building blocks of traditional Chinese architecture

tao a person's moral sense

Tien Dey Sien a series of early initiatives by a local telecommunications firm Hutchison to advertise paging service

ton kung four tiers of cantilevers in traditional Chinese architecture

tou blocks, part of *tou kung* of a traditional Chinese building

tou kung bracket sets that form the basis of structural support for a traditional Chinese building

tse fa a kind of lottery in traditional Chinese society

wet hang around with friends

yuet kuk gou tan Cantonese opera club

Local Food and Cooking (32 Instances)

chau stir-fry
  chau mihn fried noodles
  choi vegetables
  choi sum a kind of vegetables only grown in southern parts of China
  dim sum dumplings in Chinese cuisine
  lou chau dark soy sauce
  mushu roast piglets commonly served at a wedding banquet
  naaih chah tea with milk
  ngau nau beef loin
  ngau yuk / ngauh yuhk beef
  saan chau light soy sauce
  siu yuh gap roast pigeon
  sung dish as part of a meal
  tohng seui Chinese dessert
  waan yu a kind of fish usually for steaming
  yam chah / yum-cha having lunch in a Chinese restaurant

Kinship Terms (13 Instances)

ah gong grandfather
  ah tai gong father of grandfather (great grandfather)
  ah tai ma mother of grandmother (great grandmother)
  jie elder sister
  nai nai mother-in-law
  poh poh grandmother
  yeuhng neuih adopted daughter

Proper Nouns (Person; 43 Instances)

A Chiu a given name
  A Mahn a given name

Ah Ka a given name
A-mee a given name
Bo Ting a given name
Chai a surname
Fai Pang the nickname given to former governor Mr Chris Patten
Feih Liu a given name
Gong Jaahk Mahn Jiang Zemin, then president of the Communist Party of China
Gwok a surname
Hak Sing a given name
Jang Ji Mihng a surname (*Jang* or *Tsang*) plus a given name (*Ji Mihng*)
Jau Sing Chih Stephen Chow, a popular movie star in Hong Kong
Lauh Waih Hing Emily Lau, a legislative councilor
Leih a surname
Leih Yih La a surname plus a given name
Mahn a given name
Ming Sun a given name
Miu a given name
Mo a surname
Tang a surname
Wang Shi Fu name of a fortune teller
Wohng Ga Waih Wong Ka Wai, a Hong Kong film director
Wong Pak a surname plus a suffix (*baak*) for an elderly man
Wong Yaht Wah a local artiste
Yahn / Yan (Yan) a common female name
Ying Wah a given name

Proper Nouns (Place; 35 Instances)

Cheuhng Jau Cheung Chau, an outlying island in Hong Kong
Cheuhng Sihng the Great Wall in mainland China
Daaih Taahm Tai Tam, a suburb of Hong Kong
Dung Luhng Dou Tung Lung Chau, an outlying island in Hong Kong
Fuk Gin Fujian province in southern China
Gwaan Dou a place in Japan

Gwong Dung Guangdong province in southern China
Haahm Tihn Waan a place in Hong Kong
Hah Muhn Xiamen, a southern province in China
Laih Ji Gok Lai Chi Kok, a place in Hong Kong
Maahn Faht Jih a landmark of Lantau Island, which is the biggest outlying island in Hong Kong; literally meaning '10,000 buddhas monastery'
Ngau Ngak Shan name of a mountain in the New Territories of Hong Kong
Pihng Jau Ping Chau, an outlying island in Hong Kong
Sai Gung Sai Kung, a place in Hong Kong
Sai Wan Ho Sai Wan Ho, a place in Hong Kong
Sou Muih Koh-Samui, a place in Thailand
Taam Seui a place in Guangdong province of China
Tin Shau Ngam name of a convent in the New Territories of Hong Kong
Wahn Naahm Yunnan, a province in China

Proper Nouns (Organisation; 22 Instances)

Bai Shangdi Hui God Worshippers, a religious organisation
  Bou Leuhng (Guhk) Po Leung Kuk, which is one of the most established charitable organisations based locally in Hong Kong
  Chat Gei name of a shop
  Ching Wah Tsing Hua University in Beijing, China
  Chung Qil name of a Chinese-style department store
  Dung Wah Tung Wah Hospital
  Fat Tung name of a shop
  Hoh Dung name of a dormitory at the University of Hong Kong
  Ngaih Nahng name of a music company
  Tai Ping name of a shop
  Tai Wa name of a Chinese-style department store
  Youde name of a shop

Miscellaneous English Vocabulary (120 Instances)

baahk hyut bihng haemophilia
  bat pen
  beih dauh sinus
  bo sih boss
  bou sauh revenge
  cheuih yi random
  Chuen Yip Mun Pung a professional diploma
  chuhng heavy
  chyuhn syut legend
  daaih ga pronoun *we*
  daaih jyun sang post-secondary students
  deui baahk subtitles
  duhk read or study
  dung (fong) the East
  faahn hahp lunch box
  fong yihn dialects
  gau number nine
  gei gam funds
  ging seuhng often
  ging-chaat police
  Go Cup Wui Gnai Si senior accountant
  gu fan chai privatisation in China
  gwan sih military
  hoi chi to begin
  ji sih luhk instant recording
  jung chaan middle class
  jyu yahn masters
  jyun seuhng hohk yun post-secondary college
  jyun seuhng hohk yun hohk saang post-secondary college students
  keih ta the others
  laahm lihng blue-collar workers
  laahng cold

laam kauh rugby
lihng wahn soul
lohk yuh raining
lou baan boss
maahn slow
mihng sing tourist attractions
muih (muih) each
muih (yat) yaht (muih yaht) each day
muih go yahn each person
neih maaih hide
seuhng lauh seh wuih upper class
sing Form Two get promoted to Secondary Two
tight sun a replacement
tin hei weather
ting yaht tomorrow
tou earth
Wui Gai Chuen Yip professional accountancy
Wui Gnai Si accountant
yan man humanities
yat man one dollar
yih lihng lihng yat Year 2001
yihn gau sang postgraduate students
yihng san orientation day or welcoming programme for new students
ying mahn yuhn sing daaih dihp original English soundtrack or album
ying mahn / yuh deui baahk English subtitles
yuhn sing daaih dihp soundtrack

Appendix 2: Positive and Negative Keywords of Blogs in Hong Kong English

Top 150 positive keywords of GloWbE-HK (against the reference corpus GloWbE-GB)

Rank	Freq.	Keyness (LL ratio)	Positive keyword
1	17,228	73,189.252	hong
2	16,940	71,176.564	kong
3	13,614	33,210.085	china
4	5,923	27,494.286	hk
5	9,459	25,656.605	chinese
6	2,557	7769.361	beijing
7	54,654	7465.794	your
8	2,027	6789.644	louboutin
9	1,743	6569.728	yuan
10	1,768	5552.140	mainland
11	1,688	4939.204	moncler
12	1,511	4313.819	shanghai
13	1,050	3784.457	chen
14	2,283	3692.213	asia
15	1,107	3573.482	wang
16	970	3547.991	liu
17	1,061	3534.248	cher
18	782	3507.792	leung
19	1,721	3453.946	outlet
20	1,217	3400.293	li
21	793	3251.163	cantonese

(continued)

© The Author(s) 2017
M. Wong, *Hong Kong English*,
DOI 10.1057/978-1-137-51964-1

(continued)

Rank	Freq.	Keyness (LL ratio)	Positive keyword
22	2,524	3212.929	shoes
23	681	3175.242	kowloon
24	857	3058.584	zhang
25	737	3044.823	shenzhen
26	7,683	3000.750	market
27	1,486	2858.085	visa
28	1,058	2840.021	pas
29	759	2699.140	tai
30	5,818	2666.836	food
31	1,210	2632.523	enterprises
32	697	2626.993	wong
33	535	2603.309	ponyboy
34	526	2547.724	theadgear
35	4,444	2516.950	products
36	121,001	2476.289	you
37	684	2410.088	macau
38	726	2274.839	yang
39	2,989	2231.090	workers
40	27,236	2171.298	also
41	927	2165.159	jewelry
42	440	2127.649	tbeneficiary
43	1,663	2113.385	japanese
44	752	2098.777	taiwan
45	631	2093.472	chan
46	6,039	2090.275	online
47	473	2087.006	cheung
48	978	2018.145	province
49	4,923	1992.875	body
50	423	1991.503	hkd
51	590	1988.960	tang
52	513	1986.262	guangdong
53	405	1981.619	tactuality
54	48,138	1968.197	can
55	597	1936.326	abercrombie
56	3,998	1923.607	students
57	1,333	1911.217	tourism
58	3,221	1908.517	property
59	2,436	1903.835	program
60	1,295	1872.437	color
61	555	1854.426	rmb
62	2,859	1847.370	gold
63	377	1844.618	ppthe

(continued)

(continued)

Rank	Freq.	Keyness (LL ratio)	Positive keyword
64	766	1826.138	replica
65	409	1808.990	tung
66	674	1799.044	jerseys
67	609	1797.477	wu
68	4,911	1780.575	water
69	385	1778.325	chau
70	965	1769.364	wan
71	762	1753.714	pp
72	398	1745.878	mtr
73	353	1727.189	abender
74	1,121	1725.559	singapore
75	2,864	1719.830	french
76	1,248	1710.828	asian
77	5,061	1706.795	development
78	2,930	1697.524	addition
79	1,997	1694.344	fat
80	732	1681.061	vuitton
81	3,723	1643.991	air
82	7,132	1630.264	company
83	446	1627.984	guangzhou
84	438	1619.554	zhao
85	873	1592.662	bureau
86	1,802	1590.285	center
87	2203	1585.466	wine
88	336	1576.936	humoristh
89	2,472	1569.650	skin
90	397	1556.918	sade
91	373	1551.930	sai
92	1,620	1528.962	japan
93	742	1518.300	pills
94	840	1513.326	pollution
95	2,558	1501.760	insurance
96	384	1501.200	shui
97	537	1499.289	mandarin
98	866	1497.076	casino
99	1,725	1476.588	lt
100	316	1472.580	yuen
101	328	1472.447	tsang
102	394	1463.478	xu
103	377	1445.194	lam
104	373	1440.692	abounding
105	720	1434.645	handbags

(continued)

(continued)

Rank	Freq.	Keyness (LL ratio)	Positive keyword
106	536	1429.558	herbal
107	2,164	1421.665	percent
108	350	1404.513	cy
109	1,570	1403.292	restaurant
110	387	1396.633	tnt
111	307	1377.659	faustus
112	587	1363.096	abundant
113	1585	1362.396	construction
114	465	1359.364	yu
115	834	1359.187	labor
116	530	1356.445	po
117	1,968	1355.071	island
118	383	1342.994	chung
119	282	1338.417	greasers
120	7941	1322.280	high
121	2648	1317.217	prices
122	3,608	1296.923	management
123	828	1292.531	tobacco
124	315,023	1285.242	of
125	1,296	1277.113	bags
126	1,919	1271.720	cultural
127	2,692	1263.251	weight
128	805	1256.162	nike
129	304	1255.720	socs
130	266	1230.654	mainlanders
131	253	1225.011	sheung
132	295	1218.018	femi
133	351	1201.989	jiang
134	524	1199.964	nude
135	435	1193.617	lin
136	4,078	1183.533	design
137	292	1179.733	xinhua
138	1,013	1179.624	leather
139	1,476	1175.081	diet
140	320	1173.859	cheng
141	2,238	1165.751	hotel
142	3,534	1143.952	product
143	423	1142.777	casinos
144	240	1142.507	hku
145	668,579	1139.729	the
146	376	1128.244	kung
147	1,331	1123.789	enterprise

(continued)

(continued)

Rank	Freq.	Keyness (LL ratio)	Positive keyword
148	3,622	1118.522	according
149	1,148	1112.962	district
150	4,193	1109.724	industry

Top 150 negative keywords of GloWbE-HK (against the reference corpus GloWbE-GB)

Rank	Freq.	Keyness (LL ratio)	Negative keyword
1	104,189	18,520.764	i
2	108,980	7171.161	it
3	31,145	6719.822	n
4	32,189	6440.488	t
5	52	4630.870	arsenal
6	35,119	4494.057	he
7	1,849	4451.150	uk
8	126,988	4307.089	that
9	466	3950.533	league
10	198,702	3849.804	p
11	76,859	3607.461	s
12	46,785	3597.937	we
13	1,294	3533.429	players
14	47,381	3354.244	but
15	5,925	3227.960	ve
16	1,615	3133.410	season
17	22,182	3072.829	would
18	8,164	3061.045	m
19	3,335	2779.964	team
20	3,496	2718.275	game
21	59,491	2605.162	was
22	10,563	2487.159	think
23	80	2461.849	liverpool
24	771	2341.247	football
25	220	2326.888	bbc
26	25,257	2317.290	what
27	15,165	2281.811	me
28	24,215	2251.176	his
29	742	2231.743	fans
30	61,600	2180.543	have
31	97	2058.888	chelsea
32	8,222	2025.402	him
33	21,607	1989.553	who
34	19,962	1903.704	been

(continued)

(continued)

Rank	Freq.	Keyness (LL ratio)	Negative keyword
35	7	1883.043	wenger
36	934	1872.678	player
37	1716	1797.562	club
38	178	1733.939	scotland
39	108	1654.484	manchester
40	35,890	1593.468	do
41	8,131	1590.898	re
42	4,937	1578.578	d
43	903	1532.003	comment
44	28,661	1488.461	my
45	9,904	1463.317	being
46	99	1333.563	squad
47	45,221	1295.373	they
48	21,359	1250.437	had
49	32,589	1211.695	so
50	1,490	1208.039	win
51	2,095	1207.428	london
52	17	1197.305	midfield
53	401	1196.507	eu
54	3,828	1150.050	against
55	20,534	1118.471	just
56	593	1116.256	teams
57	226	1104.657	israel
58	10,989	1053.287	did
59	123	1053.198	scottish
60	1,699	1045.962	film
61	45	1027.702	nhs
62	7,583	1015.691	last
63	3,416	1013.613	play
64	1,473	1000.644	comments
65	230	986.426	premier
66	33	979.856	striker
67	20	972.354	spurs
68	96	928.614	cameron
69	6,099	928.528	something
70	826	925.120	ball
71	13,222	913.876	could
72	683	909.109	david
73	49,853	900.401	at
74	2,307	892.836	games
75	5,109	880.832	got
76	3,186	872.836	ca

(continued)

(continued)

Rank	Freq.	Keyness (LL ratio)	Negative keyword
77	84,142	871.798	on
78	6,502	844.898	say
79	1,045	838.619	played
80	929	837.695	match
81	13,446	837.345	now
82	555	833.877	britain
83	27,629	832.701	about
84	9,121	823.161	does
85	18	821.652	allah
86	879	815.302	whilst
87	10,702	809.669	back
88	3191	795.641	rather
89	245	795.404	defence
90	547	744.479	vote
91	4,504	738.746	point
92	157	738.139	champions
93	35	733.668	newcastle
94	4,790	733.318	ll
95	1,603	717.588	playing
96	1,233	714.292	england
97	6,469	714.235	why
98	10	705.357	tories
99	489	698.317	album
100	3	693.758	arsene
101	9	693.098	tottenham
102	143	686.673	wales
103	3,759	684.790	bit
104	1,276	677.333	agree
105	5	670.307	suarez
106	6	665.229	everton
107	14,588	648.435	then
108	12,346	645.759	over
109	496	645.659	debate
110	7,087	643.637	am
111	215	641.728	organisations
112	11,436	632.367	see
113	81	630.064	attacking
114	35	628.284	bristol
115	713	623.222	twitter
116	3,468	617.528	ever
117	12	616.417	savile
118	406	613.933	clubs

(continued)

(continued)

Rank	Freq.	Keyness (LL ratio)	Negative keyword
119	2,137	612.358	anyone
120	977	611.903	john
121	1,781	611.533	wrong
122	972	611.108	manager
123	10,842	609.751	know
124	8,590	608.341	going
125	5,624	606.647	never
126	18	604.867	midfielder
127	24,676	600.485	out
128	19,531	591.157	were
129	3,353	590.768	done
130	3	589.796	persie
131	18,307	589.731	them
132	1,183	587.985	goal
133	7,484	584.743	off
134	3,332	580.838	left
135	264	580.722	behaviour
136	1,602	579.035	saying
137	2,347	575.709	hope
138	372	575.633	al
139	6,564	572.233	things
140	242	570.622	realise
141	25,922	563.849	up
142	255	561.749	pitch
143	2	560.860	snp
144	31,710	560.727	there
145	19	557.550	stoke
146	1,048	555.537	evidence
147	341	551.416	organisation
148	1,186	550.002	labour
149	76	546.902	tory
150	10	544.416	theo

References

Adegbija, Efurosibina, and Janet Bello. 2001. The Semantics of 'Okay' (OK) in Nigerian English. *World Englishes* 20(1): 89–98.

Aijmer, Karin. 1979. The Function of Tag Questions in English. In *Papers from the Fifth Scandinavian Conference of Linguistics*, ed. Tore Pettersson, 9–17. Lund, Sweden: Acta Universitatis Lundensis and Stockholm: Almqvist and Wiksell.

———. 1986. Why Is *Actually* So Popular in Spoken English? In *English in Speech and Writing: A Symposium*, ed. Gunnel Tottie and Ingegerd Bäcklund, 119–129. Stockholm: Almquist and Wiksell.

———. 1996. *Conversational Routines in English*. London: Longman.

———. 2002. *English Discourse Particles: Evidence from a Corpus*. Amsterdam and Philadelphia: John Benjamins.

Algeo, John. 2006. *British or American English? A Handbook of Word and Grammar Patterns*. Cambridge: Cambridge University Press.

Ansaldo, Umberto. 2009. The Asian Typology of English: Theoretical and Methodological Considerations. *English World-Wide* 30(2): 133–148.

Anthony, Laurence. 2014. *AntConc* (Version 3.4.3) [Computer Software]. Tokyo, Japan: Waseda University. http://www.laurenceanthony.net/software.html. Accessed 14 June 2016.

Aremo, W.B. 2005. On Some Uses of Singular Collective Nouns. *English Today* 21(1): 32–55.

© The Author(s) 2017   **185**
M. Wong, *Hong Kong English*,
DOI 10.1057/978-1-137-51964-1

Ariel, Mira. 2010. *Defining Pragmatics*. New York: Cambridge University Press.

Bache, Carl, and Niels Davidsen-Nielsen. 1997. *Mastering English: An Advanced Grammar for Non-Native and Native Speakers*. Berlin and New York: Mouton de Gruyter.

Bardovi-Harlig, Kathleen, and Beverly Hartford. 1993. Learning the Rules of Academic Talk: A Longitudinal Study of Pragmatic Development. *Studies in Second Language Acquisition* 15(3): 279–304.

Bauer, Laurie. 2002. *An Introduction to International Varieties of English*. Edinburgh: Edinburgh University Press.

Bauer, Robert. 2006. The Stratification of English Loanwords in Cantonese. *Journal of Chinese Linguistics* 34(2): 172–191.

Beebe, Leslie, and Tomoko Takahashi. 1989. Do You Have a Bag? Social Status and Patterned Variation in Second Language Acquisition. In *Variation in Second Language Acquisition: Discourse and Pragmatics*, ed. Susan Gass, Carolyn Madden, Dennis Preston, and Larry Selinker, 103–125. Clevedon and Philadelphia: Multilingual Matters.

Benson, Phil. 1994. The Political Vocabulary in Hong Kong English. *Hong Kong Papers in Linguistics and Language Teaching* 17(1): 63–81.

———. 2000. Hong Kong Words: Variation and Context. *World Englishes* 19 (3): 373–380.

Biber, Douglas, Susan Conrad, and Geoffrey Leech. 2002. *Longman Student Grammar of Spoken and Written English*. Harlow, UK: Longman.

Biber, Douglas, and Jesse Egbert. 2016. Register Variation on the Searchable Web: A Multi-Dimensional Analysis. *Journal of English Linguistics* 44(2): 95–137.

Biber, Douglas, Stig Johansson, Geoffrey Leech, Susan Conrad, and Edward Finegan. 1999. *Longman Grammar of Spoken and Written English*. Harlow, UK: Longman.

Bilbow, Grahame, and Lan Li. 2001. Following Landscape . . .. *English Today* 17 (4): 27–34.

Blom, Jan-Peter, and John Gumperz. 1972. Social Meaning in Linguistic Structure: Code-Switching in Norway. In *Directions in Sociolinguistics: The Ethnography of Communication*, ed. John Gumperz and Dell Hymes, 407–434. New York: Holt, Rinehart and Winston.

Blum-Kulka, Shoshana. 1982. Learning How to Say What You Mean in a Second Language: A Study of the Speech Act Performance of Learners of Hebrew as a Second Language. *Applied Linguistics* 3(1): 29–59.

Bodman, Jean, and Miriam Eisenstein. 1988. May God Increase Your Bounty: The Expressions of Gratitude in English by Native and Non-Native Speakers. *Cross Currents* 15(1): 1–21.

Bolt, Philip, and Kingsley Bolton. 1996. The International Corpus of English in Hong Kong. In *Comparing English Worldwide: The International Corpus of English*, ed. Sidney Greenbaum, 197–214. Oxford: Clarendon Press.

Bolton, Kingsley. 2000. Researching Hong Kong English: Bibliographical Resources. *World Englishes* 19(3): 445–452.

———, ed. 2002. *Hong Kong English: Autonomy and Creativity*. Hong Kong: Hong Kong University Press.

———. 2003. *Chinese Englishes: A Sociolinguistic History*. Cambridge: Cambridge University Press.

Bolton, Kingsley, and Gerald Nelson. 2002. Analysing Hong Kong English: Sample Texts from the International Corpus of English. In *Hong Kong English: Autonomy and Creativity*, ed. Kingsley Bolton, 241–264. Hong Kong: Hong Kong University Press.

Bondi, Marina. 2010. Perspectives on Keywords and Keyness: An Introduction. In *Keyness in Texts*, ed. Marina Bondi and Mike Scott, 1–18. Amsterdam and Philadelphia: John Benjamins.

Bourhis, Richard. 1984. Cross-Cultural Communication in Montreal: Two Field Studies Since Bill 101. *International Journal of the Sociology of Language* 46(1984): 33–47.

Budge, Carol. 1989. Plural Marking in Hong Kong English. *HongKong Papers in Linguistics and Language Teaching* 12(1989): 39–47.

Cane, Graeme. 1996. Syntactic Simplification and Creativity in Spoken Brunei English. In *Language Use and Language Change in Brunei Darussalam*, ed. Peter Martin, Conrad Ozog, and Gloria Poedjosoedarmo, 209–222. Athens, Ohio: Ohio University Center for International Studies.

Carless, David. 1995. Politicised Expressions in the South China Morning Post. *English Today* 11(2): 18–22.

Cattell, Ray. 1973. Negative Transportation and Tag Questions. *Language* 49(3): 612–639.

Census & Statistics Department. 2006. Population By-Census. http://www.bycensus2006.gov.hk/en/index.htm. Accessed 14 June 2016.

———. 2011. Population Census. http://www.census2011.gov.hk/en/index.html. Accessed 14 June 2016.

———. 2014. Hong Kong Monthly Digest of Statistics: June 2014 Feature Article: Use of Language in Hong Kong in 2012. http://www.statistics.gov. hk/pub/B71406FB2014XXXXB0100.pdf Accessed 7 July 2016.

Chan, Brian Hok-shing. 1998. How Does Cantonese-English Code-Mixing Work? In *Language in Hong Kong at Century's End*, ed. Martha Pennington, 191–216. Hong Kong: Hong Kong University Press.

———. 2003. *Aspects of the Syntax, the Pragmatics and the Production of Code-Switching: Cantonese and English*. New York: Peter Lang.

———. 2007. Hybrid Language and Hybrid Identity: The Case of Cantonese-English Code-Switching in Hong Kong. In *East-West Identities: Globalisation, Localisation and Hybridisation*, ed. Chan Kwok-bun, Jan Walls, and David Hayward, 189–202. Leiden and Boston: Brill Academic Press.

Chan, Mimi, and Helen Kwok. 1985. *A Study of Lexical Borrowing from Chinese into English with Special Reference to Hong Kong*. Hong Kong: Centre of Asian Studies, University of Hong Kong.

Cheng, Stephanie Weijung. 2006. A Exploratory Cross-Sectional Study of Interlanguage Pragmatic Development of Expressions of Gratitude by Chinese Learners of English. Unpublished PhD Thesis, University of Iowa, USA.

Cheng, Winnie, and Martin Warren. 2000. The Hong Kong Corpus of Spoken English: Language Learning Through Language Description. In *Rethinking Language Pedagogy from a Corpus Perspective*, ed. Lou Burnard and Tony McEnery, 81–104. Frankfurt: Peter Lang.

———. 2001. 'She Knows About Hong Kong Than You Do Isn't It?': Tags in Hong Kong Conversational English. *Journal of Pragmatics* 33(9): 1419–1439.

Cheung, Yat-shing. 1985. Power, Solidarity and Luxury in Hong Kong: A Sociolinguistic Study. *Anthropological Linguistics* 27(2): 190–203.

Coates, Jennifer. 1996. *Women Talk*. Cambridge, MA: Blackwell.

Collins Cobuild English Grammar. 1990. London: HarperCollins.

Coulmas, Florian. 1981. 'Poison to Your Soul': Thanks and Apologies Contrastively Viewed. In *Conversational Routine: Explorations in Standardized Communication Situations and Prepatterned Speech*, ed. Florian Coulmas, 69–91. The Hague: Mouton.

Cruse, Alan. 2004. *Meaning in Language: An Introduction Semantics and Pragmatics*. Oxford: Oxford University Press.

Crystal, David. 2003. *English as a Global Language*. Cambridge and New York: Cambridge University Press.

Cummings, Patrick, and Hans-Georg Wolf. 2011. *A Dictionary of Hong Kong English: Words from the Fragrant Harbour.* Hong Kong: Hong Kong University Press.

Dahl, Östen, and Viveka Velupillai. 2008. The Past Tense. In *The World Atlas of Language Structures Online*, ed. Martin Haspelmath, Matthew S. Dryer, David Gil, and Bernard Comrie, 66. Munich: Max Planck Digital Library. http://wals.info/feature/66. Accessed 14 June 2016.

Davies, Mark. 2013. Corpus of Global Web-Based English: 1.9 Billion Words from Speakers in 20 Countries. http://corpus.byu.edu/glowbe/. Accessed 14 June 2016.

Davies, Mark, and Robert Fuchs. 2015. Expanding Horizons in the Study of World Englishes with the 1.9 Billion Word Global Web-Based English Corpus (GloWbE). *English World-Wide* 36(1): 1–28.

De Klerk, Vivian. 2005. The Use of *Actually* in Spoken Xhosa English: A Corpus Study. *World Englishes* 24(3): 275–288.

Dekeyser, Xavier, Betty Devriendt, Guy A.J. Tops, and Steven Geukens. 1999. *Foundations of English Grammar.* 5th ed. Leuven and Amersfoort: Acco.

Denke, Annika. 2009. *Nativelike Performance: A Corpus Study of Pragmatic Markers, Repairs and Repetition in Native and Non-Native English Speech.* Saarbrücken: VdmVerlag.

Depraetere, Ilse. 2003. On Verbal Concord with Collective Nouns in British English. *English Language and Linguistics* 7(1): 85–127.

Diaz Perez, Francisco Javier. 2005. The Speech Act of Thanking in English: Differences Between Native and Non-Native Speakers' Behaviour. *ES: Revista de Filologia Inglesa* 26(2005): 91–101.

Eisenstein, Miriam, and Jean Bodman. 1986. 'I Very Appreciate': Expressions of Gratitude by Native and Non-Native Speakers of American English. *Applied Linguistics* 7(2): 167–185.

———. 1993. Expressing Gratitude in American English. In *Interlanguage Pragmatics*, ed. Gabriele Kasper and Shoshana Blum-Kulka, 64–81. Oxford and New York: Oxford University Press.

Ellis, Nick. 1997. Vocabulary Acquisition: Word Structure, Collocation, Word-Class, and Meaning. In *Vocabulary: Description, Acquisition and Pedagogy*, ed. Norbert Schmitt and Michael McCarthy, 122–139. Cambridge: Cambridge University Press.

Erman, Britt, Margareta Lewis, and Lars Fant. 2013. Multiword Structures in Different Materials, and with Different Goals and Methodologies. In

Yearbook of Corpus Linguistics and Pragmatics 2013: New Domains and Methodologies, ed. Jesús Romero-Trillo, 77–103. Dordrecht: Springer.

Ervin-Tripp, Susan. 1964. An Analysis of the Interaction of Language, Topic, and Listener. *American Anthropologist* 66(Suppl. 3): 86–102.

Evans, Stephen. 2009. The Evolution of the English-Language Speech Community in Hong Kong. *English World-Wide* 30(3): 278–301.

———. 2011. Hong Kong English: The Growing Pains of a New Variety. *Asian Englishes* 14(1): 22–45.

———. 2015. Testing the Dynamic Model: The Evolution of the Hong Kong English Lexicon (1858–2012). *Journal of English Linguistics* 43(3): 175–200.

Fishman, Joshua. 1965. Who Speaks What Language to Whom and When? *La Linguistique* 1(2): 67–88.

———. 1972. Domains and the Relationship Between Micro- and Macro-Sociolinguistics. In *Directions in Sociolinguistics: The Ethnography of Communication*, ed. John Gumperz and Dell Hymes, 435–453. New York: Holt, Rinehart and Winston.

———. 1975. The Relationship Between Micro- and Macro-Sociolinguistics in the Study of Who Speaks What Language to Whom and When. In *Bilingualism in the Barrio*, ed. Joshua Fishman, Robert Cooper, and Roxana Ma, 2nd ed., 583–603. The Hague: Mouton.

Fu, Gail. 1975. A Hong Kong Perspective: English Language Learning and the Chinese Context. Unpublished PhD Dissertation, University of Michigan, USA.

Gibbons, John. 1983. Attitudes Towards Languages and Code-Mixing in Hong Kong. *Journal of Multilingual and Multicultural Development* 4(2–3): 129–147.

———. 1987. *Code-Mixing and Code Choice: A Hong Kong Case Study*. Clevedon and Philadelphia: Multilingual Matters.

Giles, Howard, Richard Bourhis, and Donald Taylor. 1977. Towards a Theory of Language in Ethnic Group Relations. In *Language, Ethnicity and Intergroup Relations*, ed. Howard Giles, 307–348. London: Academic Press.

Giles, Howard, Nikolas Coupland, and Justine Coupland. 1991. Accommodation Theory: Communication, Context, and Consequence. In *Contexts of Accommodation: Developments in Applied Sociolinguistics*, ed. Howard Giles, Nikolas Coupland, and Justine Coupland, 1–68. Cambridge: Cambridge University Press.

Giles, Howard, and Philip Smith. 1979. Accommodation Theory: Optimal Levels of Convergence. In *Language and Social Psychology*, ed. Howard Giles and Robert St. Clair, 45–65. Oxford: Blackwell.

Gisborne, Nikolas. 2000. Relative Clauses in Hong Kong English. *World Englishes* 19(3): 357–371.

———. 2009. Aspects of the Morphosyntactic Typology of Hong Kong English. *English World-Wide* 30(2): 149–169.

Golato, Andrea. 2003. Studying Compliment Responses: A Comparison of DCTs and Recordings of Naturally Occurring Talk. *Applied Linguistics* 21 (1): 90–121.

Granger, Sylviane. 1998. Prefabricated Patterns in Advanced EFL Writing: Collocations and Formulae. In *Phraseology: Theory, Analysis and Applications*, ed. A.P. Cowie, 145–160. Oxford: Oxford University Press.

Greenbaum, Sidney. 1996. *Oxford English Grammar*. Oxford: Oxford University Press.

Grieve, Jack, Douglas Biber, Eric Friginal, and Tatianna Nekrasova. 2011. Variation Among Blogs: A Multi-Dimensional Analysis. In *Genres on the Web: Corpus Studies and Computational Models*, ed. Alexander Mehler, Serge Sharoff, and Marina Santini, 303–322. New York: Springer-Verlag.

Groves, Julie. 2012. The Issue of Representativeness in Hong Kong English. *Asian Englishes* 15(1): 28–45.

Gumperz, John. 1964. Linguistic and Social Interaction in Two Communities. *American Anthropologist* 66(Suppl. 3): 137–153.

———. 1982. *Discourse Strategies*. New York: Cambridge University Press.

Han, Chung-hye. 1992. A Comparative Study of Compliment Responses: Korean Females in Korean Interactions and in English Interactions. *Working Papers in Educational Linguistics* 8(2): 17–31.

Herring, Susan, and John Paolillo. 2006. Gender and Genre Variation in Weblogs. *Journal of Sociolinguistics* 10(4): 439–459.

Herring, Susan, Lois Ann Scheidt, Inna Kouper, and Elijah Wright. 2007. A Longitudinal Content Analysis of Weblogs: 2003–2004. In *Blogging, Citizenship and the Future of Media*, ed. Mark Tremayne, 3–20. London: Routledge.

Herring, Susan, Lois Ann Scheidt, Elijah Wright, and Sabrina Bonus. 2004. Bridging the Gap: A Genre Analysis of Weblogs. In *Proceedings of the 37th Hawaii International Conference on System Sciences*, 101–111. Los Alamitos, CA: IEEE Computer Society Press.

———. 2005. Weblogs as a Bridging Genre. *Information, Technology and People* 18(2): 142–171.

Hinkel, Eli. 1994. Pragmatics of Interaction: Expressing Thanks in a Second Language. *Applied Language Learning* 5(1): 73–91.

Hoffmann, Sebastian, Anne-Katrin Blass, and Joybrato Mukherjee. 2014. Canonical Tag Questions in Asian Englishes: Forms, Functions, and Frequencies in Hong Kong English, Indian English, and Singapore English. In *The Oxford Handbook of World Englishes*, ed. Markku Filppula, Juhani Klemola, and Devyani Sharma. Oxford: Oxford University Press.

Holmes, Janet. 1983. The Functions of Tag Questions. *English Language Research Journal* 3(1983): 40–65.

———. 1984. Modifying Illocutionary Force. *Journal of Pragmatics* 8(3): 345–365.

———. 1995. *Women, Men and Politeness*. White Plains, NY: Longman.

Hu, Jianhua, Haihua Pan, and Liejiong Xu. 2001. Is There a Finite vs. Non-Finite Distinction in Chinese? *Linguistics* 39(6): 1117–1148.

Huddleston, Rodney. 1970. Two Approaches to the Analysis of Tags. *Journal of Linguistics* 6(1970): 215–222.

———. 1988. *English Grammar: An Outline*. Cambridge: Cambridge University Press.

Huddleston, Rodney, and Geoffrey Pullum. 2002. *The Cambridge Grammar of the English Language*. Cambridge: Cambridge University Press.

Hundt, Marianne. 2006. The Committee Has/Have Decided . . . on Concord Patterns with Collective Nouns in Inner- and Outer-Circle Varieties of English. *Journal of English Linguistics* 34(3): 206–232.

Hung, Tony. 2000. Towards a Phonology of Hong Kong English. *World Englishes* 19(3): 337–356.

Hussain, Zahida, and Muhammad Asim Mahmood. 2014. Invariant Tag Questions in Pakistani English: A Comparsion with Native and Other Non-Native Englishes. *Asian Englishes* 16(3): 229–238.

Hymes, Dell. 1967. Models of the Interaction of Language and Social Setting. *Journal of Social Issues* 23(2): 8–28.

———. 1971. Sociolinguistics and the Ethnography of Speaking. In *Social Anthropology and Language*, ed. Edwin Ardener, 47–93. London: Tavistock.

Ide, Risako. 1998. 'Sorry for Your Kindness': Japanese Interactional Ritual in Public Discourse. *Journal of Pragmatics* 29(5): 509–529.

Jacobsson, Mattias. 2002. *Thank You* and *Thanks* in Early Modern English. *ICAME Journal* 26(2002): 63–80.

Jenkins, Jennifer. 2009. *World Englishes: A Resource Book for Students*. 2nd ed. London and New York: Routledge.

Johnson, Robert K. 1994. Language Policy and Planning in Hong Kong. *Annual Review of Applied Linguistics* 14(1): 177–199.

Joseph, John. 1996. English in Hong Kong: Emergence and Decline. *Current Issues in Language and Society* 3(2): 166–179.

———. 1997. English in Hong Kong: Emergence and Decline. In *One Country, Two Systems, Three Languages: A Survey of Changing Language Use in Hong Kong*, ed. Sue Wright and Helen Kelly-Holmes, 60–79. Cleveon: Multilingual Matters.

———. 2004. *Language and Identity: National, Ethnic, Religious*. Basingstoke: Palgrave Macmillan.

Kachru, Braj. 1985. Standards, Codification and Sociolinguistic Realism: The English Language in the Outer Circle. In *English in the World: Teaching and Learning the Language and Literatures*, ed. Randolph Quirk and Henry Widdowson, 11–36. Cambridge: Cambridge University Press.

———. 1992. World Englishes: Approaches, Issues and Resources. *Language Teaching* 25(1): 1–14.

Kachru, Yamuna, and Cecil Nelson. 2006. *World Englishes in Asian Contexts*. Hong Kong: Hong Kong University Press.

Kachru, Yamuna, and Larry Smith. 2008. *Cultures, Contexts, and World Englishes*. New York and London: Routledge.

Kimura, Kazumi. 1994. The Multiple Functions of *Sumimasen*. *Issues in Applied Linguistics* 5(2): 279–302.

Kirkpatrick, Andy. 2007. *World Englishes: Implications for International Communication and English Language Teaching*. Cambridge: Cambridge University Press.

Kortmann, Bernd, and Benedikt Szmrecsanyi. 2004. Global Synopsis: Morphological and Syntactic Variation in English. In *A Handbook of Varieties of English*, Vol. 2: *Morphology and Syntax*, ed. Bernd Kortmann, Kate Burridge, Rajend Mesthrie, Edgar W. Schneider, and Clive Upton, 1142–1202. Berlin and New York: Mouton de Gruyter.

Kramsch, Claire. 1998. *Language and Culture*. Oxford: Oxford University Press.

Krishnamurthy, Sandeep. 2002. The Multidimensionality of Blog Conversations: The Virtual Enactment of September 11. Paper presented at Internet Research 3.0, Maastricht, The Netherlands.

Kumatoridani, Tetsuo. 1999. Alternation and Co-Occurrence in Japanese Thanks. *Journal of Pragmatics* 31(5): 623–642.

Kwok, Shirley. 1997. New Rule Will Halve Schools Using English. *South China Morning Post*, 22 March, p. 7.

Lai, Mee-ling. 2009. 'I Love Cantonese, But I Want English'—A Qualitative Account of Hong Kong Students' Language Attitudes. *The Asia-Pacific Education Researchers* 18(1): 79–92.

Lau, Chi-kuen. 1995. Language of the Future. *South China Morning Post*, 18 September, p. 19.

Lee, Jackie. 2001. Functions of *Need* in Australian English and Hong Kong English. *World Englishes* 20(2): 133–143.

———. 2004. On the Usage of *Have, Dare, Need, Ought To* and *Used To* in Australian English and Hong Kong English. *World Englishes* 23(4): 501–513.

Leech, Geoffrey. 1983. *Principles of Pragmatics*. London: Longman.

———. 2001. The Role of Frequency in ELT: New Corpus Evidence Brings a Re-Appraisal. *Foreign Language Teaching and Research* 33(5): 328–339.

———. 2006. *A Glossary of English Grammar*. Edinburgh: Edinburgh University Press.

Leech, Geoffrey, and Jan Svartvik. 1994. *A Communicative Grammar of English*. 2nd ed. London and New York: Longman.

Levin, Magnus. 2001. *Agreement with Collective Nouns in English*. (Lund Studies in English, 103). Lund, Sweden: Lund University.

Levinson, Stephen. 1983. *Pragmatics*. Cambridge: Cambridge University Press.

Li, Charles, and Sandra Thompson. 1990. Chinese. In *The Major Languages of East and South-East Asia*, ed. Bernard Comrie, 2nd ed., 83–105. London: Routledge.

Li, David C.S. 1996. *Issues in Bilingualism and Biculturalism: A Hong Kong Case Study*. New York: Peter Lang.

———. 1998. The Plight of the Purist. In *Language in Hong Kong at Century's End*, ed. Martha Pennington, 161–190. Hong Kong: Hong Kong University Press.

———. 1999. The Functions and Status of English in Hong Kong: A Post-1997 Update. *English World-Wide* 20(1): 67–110.

———. 2003. Code Mixing Between Hong Kong Cantonese and English. *Foreign Language Teaching and Research* 35(1): 13–19.

Li, David C.S., and Alice Y.W. Chan. 1999. Helping Teachers Correct Structural and Lexical English Errors. *Hong Kong Journal of Applied Linguistics* 4(1): 79–101.

Lim, Lisa. 2009. Revisiting Prosody: (Some) New Englishes as Tone Languages? *English World-Wide* 30(2): 218–239.

Lin, Yen-Liang. 2013. Discourse Functions of Recurrent Multi-Word Sequences in Online and Spoken Intercultural Communication. In *Yearbook of Corpus*

Linguistics and Pragmatics 2013: New Domains and Methodologies, ed. Jesús Romero-Trillo, 105–129. Dordrecht: Springer.

Linguistic Society of Hong Kong. 1997. *Jyut6 ping3* [Cantonese Romanisation Scheme]. Hong Kong: Linguistic Society of Hong Kong. (In Chinese).

Low, Winnie W.M., and Dan Lu. 2006. Persistent Use of Mixed Code: An Exploration of Its Functions in Hong Kong Schools. *The International Journal of Bilingual Education and Bilingualism* 9(2): 181–204.

Luke, Dan, and Jack Richards. 1982. English in Hong Kong: Functions and Status. *English World-Wide* 3(1): 47–64.

Luke, Kang-Kwong. 1998. Why Two Languages Might Be Better Than One: Motivations of Language Mixing in Hong Kong. In *Language in Hong Kong at Century's End*, ed. Martha Pennington, 145–159. Hong Kong: Hong Kong University Press.

Martin, Peter. 2005. Language Shift and Code-Mixing: A Case Study from Northern Borneo. *Australian Journal of Linguistics* 25(1): 109–125.

Matthews, Stephen. 2006. On Serial Verb Constructions in Cantonese. In *Serial Verbs: A Cross-Linguistic Typology*, ed. Alexandra Y. Aikhenvald and R.M.W. Dixon, 69–87. Oxford: Oxford University Press.

Matthews, Stephen, and Virginia Yip. 1994. *Cantonese: A Comprehensive Grammar*. London and New York: Routledge.

———. 2011. *Cantonese: A Comprehensive Grammar*. 2nd ed. London and New York: Routledge.

McArthur, Tom. 1987. The English Languages? *English Today* 3(3): 9–13.

———. 2002. *The Oxford Guide to World English*. Oxford and New York: Oxford University Press.

McEnery, Tony, Richard Xiao, and Tono Yukio. 2006. *Corpus-Based Language Studies: An Advanced Resource Book*. London and New York: Routledge.

McGregor, William. 1985. The English 'Tag Question': A New Analysis, Is(n't) It? In *On Subject and Theme: A Discourse Functional Perspective*, ed. Ruqaiya Hasan and Peter Fries, 91–121. Amsterdam: John Benjamins.

Melchers, Gunnel, and Philip Shaw. 2003. *World Englishes: An Introduction*. London: Arnold.

Mesthrie, Rajend. 2004. Introduction: Varieties of English in Africa and South and Southeast Asia. In *A Handbook of Varieties of English*, Vol. 2: *Morphology and Syntax*, ed. Bernd Kortmann, Kate Burridge, Rajend Mesthrie, Edgar W. Schneider, and Clive Upton, 805–812. Berlin: Mouton de Gruyter.

Miller, Carolyn, and Dawn Shepherd. 2004. Blogging as Social Action: A Genre Analysis of the Weblog. *The University of Minnesota Digital Conservancy.* http://conservancy.umn.edu/handle/11299/172818. Accessed 14 June 2016.

Mukherjee, Joybrato, and Marianne Hundt, eds. 2011. *Exploring Second-Language Varieties of English and Learner Englishes: Bridging a Paradigm Gap.* Amsterdam and Philadelphia: John Benjamins.

Mundy, John. 1978. *Communicative Syllabus Design.* Cambridge: Cambridge University Press.

Muñoa, Inma. 1997. Pragmatic Functions of Code-Switching Among Basque-Spanish Bilinguals. In *Actas del I Simposio internacional sobre bilingüismo* [Proceedings of the First International Symposium on Bilingualism], 528–541. http://webs.uvigo.es/ssl/actas1997/04/Munhoa.pdf. Accessed 14 June 2016.

Myers-Scotton, Carol. 1988. Code Switching as Indexical of Social Negotiations. In *Codeswitching: Anthropological and Sociolinguistic Perspectives*, ed. Monica Heller, 151–186. Berlin: Gruyter.

———. 1998. A Theoretical Introduction to the Markedness Model. In *Codes and Consequences: Choosing Linguistic Varieties*, ed. Carol Myers-Scotton, 18–38. New York: Oxford University Press.

———. 1999. Explaining the Role of Norms and Rationality in Codeswitching. *Journal of Pragmatics* 32(9): 1259–1271.

Myers-Scotton, Carol, and Agnes Bolonyai. 2001. Calculating Speakers: Codeswitching in a Rational Choice Model. *Language in Society* 30(1): 1–28.

Nässlin, Siv. 1984. *The English Tag Question: A Study of Sentences Containing Tags of the Type Isn't It?, Is It?* (Stockholm Studies in English, 60). Stockholm: Almqvist and Wiksell.

Nattinger, James, and Jeanette DeCarrico. 1992. *Lexical Phrases and Language Teaching.* Oxford: Oxford University Press.

Nelson, Gerald. 1996. The Design of the Corpus. In *Comparing English Worldwide: The International Corpus of English*, ed. Sidney Greenbaum, 27–35. Oxford: Clarendon Press.

———. 2006a. *The ICE Hong Kong Corpus: User Manual.* London: University College London.

———. 2006b. World Englishes and Corpora Studies. In *The Handbook of World Englishes*, ed. Braj Kachru, Yamuna Kachru, and Cecil Nelson, 733–750. Malden, MA and Oxford: Blackwell.

———. 2015. Response to Mark Davies and Robert Fuchs, Expanding Horizons in the Study of World Englishes with the 1.9 Billion Word Global Web-Based English Corpus (GloWbE). *English World-Wide* 36(1): 38–40.

Noël, Dirk, and Johan Van der Auwera. 2015. Recent Quantitative Changes in the Use of Modals and Quasi-Modals in the Hong Kong, British and American Printed Press: Exploring the Potential of Factiva® for the Diachronic Investigation of World Englishes. In *Grammatical Change in English World-Wide*, ed. Peter Collins, 437–464. Amsterdam and Philadelphia: John Benjamins.

Oh, Sun-Young. 2000. *Actually* and *In Fact* in American English: A Data-Based Analysis. *English Language and Linguistics* 4(2): 243–268.

Ooi, Vincent B.Y., and Peter K.W. Tan. 2014. Facebook, Linguistic Identity and Hybridity in Singapore. In *The Global-Local Interface and Hybridity: Exploring Language and Identity*, ed. Rani Rubdy and Lubna Alsagoff, 225–244. Bristol, Buffalo and Toronto: Multilingual Matters.

Ooi, Vincent B.Y., Peter K.W. Tan, and Andy K.L. Chiang. 2007. Analysing Personal Weblogs in Singapore English: The WMatrix Approach. In *eVarieng* (Journal of the Research Unit for Variation, Contacts, and Change in English), Vol. 2: *Towards Multimedia in Corpus Studies*. Finland: University of Helsinki. http://www.helsinki.fi/varieng/series/volumes/02/ooi_et_al/. Accessed 14 June 2016.

Östman, Jan Ola. 1981. A Functional Approach to English Tags. *Studia Anglica Posnaniensia* 13(1981): 3–16.

Pang, Terence. 2003. Hong Kong English: A Stillborn Variety? *English Today* 19 (2): 12–18.

Parviainen, Hanna. 2016. The Invariant Tag *Isn't It* in Asian Englishes. *World Englishes* 35(1): 98–117.

Peng, Long, and Jean Ann. 2004. Obstruent Voicing and Devoicing in the English of Cantonese Speakers from Hong Kong. *World Englishes* 23(4): 535–564.

Pennington, Martha, and Francis Yue. 1994. English and Chinese in Hong Kong: Pre-1997 Language Attitudes. *World Englishes* 13(1): 1–20.

Potts, Amanda, and Paul Baker. 2012. Does Semantic Tagging Identify Cultural Change in British and American English? *International Journal of Corpus Linguistics* 17(3): 295–324.

Prodromou, Luke. 2008. *English as a Lingua Franca: A Corpus-Based Analysis*. London: Continuum.

Pushmann, Cornelius. 2007a. Blogs or Flogs? Genre Conventions and Linguistic Practices in Corporate Web Logs. Invited Talk presented at the Telematica Instituut, Enschede, The Netherlands. http://www.slideshare.net/coffee001/blogs-or-flogs-genre-conventions-and-linguistic-practices-in-corporate-web-logs/. Accessed 14 June 2016.

———. 2007b. Corpora, Blogs and Linguistic Variation—Arguments for Using Structured Web Data in Corpus Development. Invited Talk presented at the University of Paderborn, Germany. http://www.slideshare.net/coffee001/corpora-blogs-and-linguistic-variation-paderborn. Accessed 14 June 2016.

Qian, David. 2008. English Language Assessment in Hong Kong: A Survey of Practices, Developments and Issues. *Language Testing* 25(1): 85–110.

Quirk, Randolph, Sidney Greenbaum, Geoffrey Leech, and Jan Svartvik. 1985. *A Comprehensive Grammar of the English Language*. London: Longman.

Rayson, Paul. 2008. From Key Words to Key Semantic Domains. *International Journal of Corpus Linguistics* 13(4): 519–549.

Rayson, Paul, Dawn Archer, Scott Piao, and Tony McEnery. 2004. The UCREL Semantic Analysis System. In *Proceedings of the Workshop on Beyond Named Entity Recognition Semantic Labelling for NLP Tasks in Association with 4th International Conference on Language Resources and Evaluation (LREC 2004)*, 25th May 2004, Lisbon, Portugal, pp. 7–12.

Schauer, Gila, and Svenja Adolphs. 2006. Expressions of Gratitude in Corpus and DCT Data: Vocabulary, Formulaic Sequences, and Pedagogy. *System* 34(1): 119–134.

Schmitt, Norbert, and Ronald Carter. 2004. Formulaic Sequences in Action. In *Formulaic Sequences: Acquisition, Processing and Use*, ed. Norbert Schmitt, 1–22. Amsterdam and Philadelphia: John Benjamins.

Schneider, Edgar. 2003. The Dynamics of New Englishes: From Identity Construction to Dialect Birth. *Language* 79(2): 233–281.

———. 2007. *Postcolonial English: Varieties Around the World*. Cambridge: Cambridge University Press.

Scott, Mike. 2010. Introduction to WordSmith Tools. http://www.lexically.net/downloads/version5/HTML/index.html. Accessed 14 June 2016.

Searle, John. 1969. *Speech Acts: An Essay in the Philosophy of Language*. Cambridge: Cambridge University Press.

Setter, Jane. 2006. Speech Rhythm in World Englishes: The Case of Hong Kong. *TESOL Quarterly* 40(4): 763–782.

Setter, Jane, Cathy Wong, and Brian Chan. 2010. *Hong Kong English*. Edinburgh: Edinburgh University Press.

Sinclair, John. 1991. *Corpus, Concordance, Collocation.* Oxford: Oxford University Press.

Smith, Larry. 1987. Introduction: Discourse Strategies and Cross-Cultural Communication. In *Discourse Across Cultures: Strategies in World Englishes,* ed. Larry Smith, 1–6. New York: Prentice Hall.

Smith, Nicholas, Sebastian Hoffmann, and Paul Rayson. 2008. Corpus Tools and Methods, Today and Tomorrow: Incorporating Linguists' Manual Annotations. *Literary and Linguistic Computing* 23(2): 163–180.

Stenström, Anna-Brita. 1997. Tags in Teenage Talk. In *From Ælfric to the New York Times: Studies in English Corpus Linguistics,* ed. Udo Fries, Viviane Müller, and Peter Schneider, 139–147. Amsterdam: Rodopi.

———. 2005. Teenagers' Tags in London and Madrid. In *Contexts—Historical, Social, Linguistic* (Studies in Celebration of Toril Swan), ed. Kevin McCafferty, Tove Bull, and Kristin Killie, 279–291. Bern, Switzerland: Peter Lang.

Stibbard, Richard. 2004. The Spoken English of Hong Kong: A Study of Co-Occurring Segmental Errors. *Language, Culture and Curriculum* 17(2): 127–142.

Strevens, Peter. 1980. *Teaching English as an International Language.* Oxford: Pergamon.

Suárez-Gómez, Cristina. 2014. Relative Clauses in Southeast Asian Englishes. *Journal of English Linguistics* 42(3): 245–268.

Swan, Michael. 1995. *Practical English Usage.* 2nd ed. Oxford: Oxford University Press.

Taglicht, Joseph. 2001. Actually, There's More to It Than Meets the Eye. *English Language and Linguistics* 5(1): 1–16.

Takahashi, Mariko. 2014. A Comparative Study of Tag Questions in Four Asian Englishes from a Corpus-Linguistic Approach. *Asian Englishes* 16(2): 101–124.

Thomas, Jenny. 1983. Cross-Cultural Pragmatic Failure. *Applied Linguistics* 4(2): 91–112.

Todd, Loreto, and Ian Hancock. 1986. *International English Usage.* London: Groom Helm.

Tottie, Gunnel, and Sebastian Hoffmann. 2006. Tag Questions in British and American English. *Journal of English Linguistics* 34(4): 283–311.

Trudgill, Peter, and Jean Hannah. 2002. *International English: A Guide to the Varieties of Standard English.* 4th ed. London: Arnold.

Tsui, Amy B.M., and David Bunton. 2000. The Discourse and Attitudes of English Language Teachers in Hong Kong. In *Hong Kong English: Autonomy and Creativity*, ed. Kingsley Bolton, 287–303. Hong Kong: Hong Kong University Press.

Werner, Valentin. 2013. Temporal Adverbials and the Present Perfect/Past Tense Alternation. *English World-Wide* 34(2): 202–240.

Wolf, Hans-Georg, and Thomas Chan. 2016. Understanding Asia by Means of Cognitive Sociolinguistics and Cultural Linguistics—The Example of GHOSTS in Hong Kong English. In *Communicating with Asia: The Future of English as a Global Language*, ed. Gerhard Leitner, Azirah Hashim, and Hans-Georg Wolf, 249–266. Cambridge: Cambridge University Press.

Wong, Cathy, Robert Bauer, and Zoe Lam. 2007. The Integration of English Loanwords in Hong Kong Cantonese. Paper presented at the 17th Annual Meeting of the Southeast Asian Linguistics Society (SEALSXVII), 31 August–2 September 2007, University of Maryland, USA.

Wong, May L-Y. 2007. Tag Questions in Hong Kong English: A Corpus-Based Study. *Asian Englishes* 10(1): 44–61.

———. 2009. *Committee, Staff, Council,* etc.: A Corpus Analysis of Collective Nouns in Hong Kong English. *Asian Englishes* 12(1): 4–19.

———. 2010. Expressions of Gratitude by Hong Kong Speakers of English: Research from the International Corpus of English in Hong Kong (ICE-HK). *Journal of Pragmatics* 42(5): 1243–1257.

Wong, May L-Y. 2012. Hong Kong English. In *The Mouton World Atlas of Variation in English*, ed. Bernd Kortmann and Kerstin Lunkenheimer, 548–561. Berlin and New York: Mouton de Gruyter.

Wong, Nick, Alfred Tsang, and Pedro Lok. 2016. The Emergence of an Overnight Success of the 'Kongish' Identity: How the Basilect Hong Kong English Becomes Prominently Preferred as a Discernible Trend on Facebook. Paper presented at *Sociolinguistics Symposium 21*, 15–18 June 2016, Universidad de Murcia, Spain.

Wray, Alison. 2000. Formulaic Sequences in Second Language Teaching: Principle and Practice. *Applied Linguistics* 21(4): 463–489.

———. 2002. *Formulaic Language and the Lexicon.* Cambridge: Cambridge University Press.

Yao, Xinyue. 2016. Cleft Constructions in Hong Kong English. *English World-Wide* 37(2): 197–220.

Yates, Lynda. 2004. The 'Secret Rules of Language': Tackling Pragmatics in the Classroom. *Prospect* 19(1): 3–21.

Yau, Frances Man-siu. 1997. Code Switching and Language Choice in the Hong Kong Legislative Council. *Journal of Multilingual and Multicultural Development* 18(1): 40–53.

Yau, Man-siu. 1993. Functions of Two Codes in Hong Kong Chinese. *World Englishes* 12(1): 25–33.

Yu, Ming-chung. 1999. Cross-Cultural and Interlanguage Pragmatics: Developing Communicative Competence in a Second Language. Unpublished PhD Thesis, Harvard University, USA.

Yuan, Yi. 2001. An Inquiry into Empirical Pragmatics Data-Gathering Methods: Written DCTs, Oral DCTs, Field Notes, and Natural Conversation. *Journal of Pragmatics* 33(2): 271–292.

Index

Note: Page numbers followed by "n" refers to notes.

© The Author(s) 2017
M. Wong, *Hong Kong English*,
DOI 10.1057/978-1-137-51964-1

GPSR Compliance
The European Union's (EU) General Product Safety Regulation (GPSR) is a set
of rules that requires consumer products to be safe and our obligations to
ensure this.

If you have any concerns about our products, you can contact us on

ProductSafety@springernature.com

In case Publisher is established outside the EU, the EU authorized
representative is:

Springer Nature Customer Service Center GmbH
Europaplatz 3
69115 Heidelberg, Germany